T0128539

"A smart and stylish cautionary tale of an artist who gets caught up in the savagery of her own art." —*Variety*

"Aim[ing] for tangled Pynchon-esque surrealism . . . Callaghan's script abounds with cleverness." —*The New Yorker*

"Callaghan has a vision that is clear, individual, and hard as the marble her leading character . . . claims as artistic capital. This is a smart writer unafraid of blood." —*Stage Voices*

THAT PRETTY PRETTY; OR, THE RAPE PLAY

"Raunchy, savvy . . . the twisted, caffeinated world of the show imagines the collective unconscious of a culture where girls never stop going wild . . . [Callaghan] push[es] her audience's buttons with an aggresssive treatment of some of the darker corners of the human psyche." —*The New York Times*

"Funny, scary, messy, and forthrightly feminist." —*Village Voice*

"A submersion in the anarchy of ambivalence: variously a rant, a riff, a rumble—about our notions of naturalism, objectification, perversity, and beauty . . . There's sass and sarcasm in Callaghan's high-energy punk writing." —*The New Yorker*

"Sheila Callaghan seems to have put third-wave feminism, Gen-Y gender confusion and macho writerly clichés in a blender set to high speed. Her manic, angry, deftly constructed *That Pretty Pretty; or, the Rape Play* whipsaws between laughs and squirms as Callaghan trawls the mucky depths of male-constructed femininity." —*Time Out New York*

Justine Cooper

Sheila Callaghan

LASCIVIOUS SOMETHING · ROADKILL CONFIDENTIAL ·
THAT PRETTY PRETTY; OR, THE RAPE PLAY

SHEILA CALLAGHAN's plays include *Scab*, *Crawl*, *Fade to White*, *Crumble (Lay Me Down, Justin Timberlake)*, *We Are Not These Hands*, *Dead City*, *Kate Crackernuts*, and *Fever/Dream*. Her work has been published by Samuel French and her monologues can be found in various anthologies. Callaghan's plays have been produced and developed with Soho Rep, Playwrights Horizons, South Coast Repertory, Actor's Theater of Louisville, New Georges, Woolly Mammoth, and Rattlestick Playwright's Theater, among others, as well as internationally. She is the recipient of the Princess Grace Award for emerging artists, a Jerome Fellowship from the Playwright's Center in Minneapolis, a MacDowell Residency, a 2005 Cherry Lane Mentorship Fellowship, the Susan Smith Blackburn Prize, and the prestigious Whiting Writers' Prize. She has received grants from NYFA, NYSCA, and the MAP Foundation, in addition to commissions from Playwrights Horizons, South Coast Repertory, the Playwright's Foundation, Clubbed Thumb, and EST/Sloan. She has taught playwriting at various colleges including Columbia University and the University of Rochester, and she is currently on the faculty at Spalding University's MFA program in creative writing. Callaghan is a resident artist at New Dramatists, an affiliated artist with Clubbed Thumb, and a member of the Obie-winning playwright's organization 13P. She is also a writer on the Showtime series *The United States of Tara*. Callaghan divides her time between Brooklyn and Los Angeles.

LASCIVIOUS
SOMETHING

★

ROADKILL
CONFIDENTIAL

★

THAT PRETTY
PRETTY;
OR,
THE RAPE
PLAY

LASCIVIOUS SOMETHING

★

ROADKILL CONFIDENTIAL

★

THAT PRETTY PRETTY; OR, THE RAPE PLAY

SHEILA CALLAGHAN

Soft Skull Press

Library of Congress Cataloging-in-Publication Data is available.

ISBN 978-1-59376-414-2

Cover design by Gretchen Achilles
Interior design by Neuwirth & Associates, Inc.
Printed in the United States of America

Soft Skull Press
New York, NY

www.softskull.com

To my husband, Sophocles

CONTENTS

PREFACE

xiii

★

LASCIVIOUS
SOMETHING

1

★

ROADKILL
CONFIDENTIAL

109

★

THAT PRETTY
PRETTY;
OR,
THE RAPE
PLAY

229

★

ACKNOWLEDGMENTS

316

PREFACE

I am absolutely humbled to write this preface for my first collection of plays. I feel so grateful to have my work recognized in this way—though it's a bit daunting to attempt to justify the existence of such a collection. It assumes I am comfortable with the premise that these plays a) belong together, b) are important enough to be examined, and c) identify me as a writer who has a great enough body of work that pieces may be extracted and compiled. Which I am not—comfortable, that is. But I shall sally forth regardless.

I bore easily. This is what I tell people when they ask me about the stylistic leaps in my plays, or my flights into fanciful language, or why I toy around with ideas that are too big for my beady little mind. It takes a lot of concentration (or a reality television show) for me to stay still for any length of time. So basically, my aim is to write something I could actually sit through without clawing the flesh off my palms.

I don't know if the plays in this collection achieve that goal for everyone else. Hopefully they are entertaining for a percentage of the folks who endeavor to sit or read through them. I see my role on this planet as that of a storyteller and an entertainer, and if I am doing neither of these well then I'm failing at life. Or at least, I suck at my job and should find another one.

But let's assume for a moment I don't suck, and that the plays in this collection beg further scrutiny. They may not be linked thematically, but they all express my chronic condition of restlessness and fear and anxiety and curiosity and dissatisfaction (which of course are the real truths behind my "boredom"). They also reveal filaments of the topics that compel me: sex, language, dishonesty, heartbreak, filth, anger, justice, art, TV, the Internet, celebrity, poetry. The order of these interests depends on my mood—or more accurately, on what each play asks me to pay attention to while I'm writing it.

With *Lascivious Something* I wanted to craft a love story that mirrored the death of American political idealism, using the 1980 election of Ronald Reagan as a backdrop. I found a vineyard to be an apt setting, as the fecundity and promise and disappointment built into the growing cycle can serve as a metaphor for our relationship to our past, whether personal or political—though as they say, the personal *is* political. I also wanted to write a big, honking Greek tragedy, for which I blame my husband, Sophocles—he's the one who dragged me to his family's land in Greece one impossibly hot summer and made me fall crazily and drunkenly in love with him. And finally, I was interested in exploring the metaphysical map of the choices we make (and don't make), and the ripples these may cause.

For *Roadkill Confidential* I researched work by the Critical Art Ensemble, a performance- and installation-art collective focused on the intersections between art, critical theory, technology, and political activism. In the spring of 2004, Stephen Kurtz, a founding member of the group, was detained without charge due to suspicions aroused by his artwork, which often uses biological specimens, including mock pathogens, and had run afoul of terrorism legislation. He was ultimately proven innocent of any threatening activity, but his case made me ponder the intersection of art and fear. When art provokes terror, is that provocation personal or global? When the goal of the art is to incite mass fear and hysteria, is the difference between art and terrorism purely contextual? And when violent acts are committed in service of the "greater good," what is the moral obligation of those who commit such acts—to take responsibility for the acts themselves, or to justify the goodness of the goals? Or both? This play hopes to ask those questions, then flee hysterically when it realizes there are no answers.

That Pretty Pretty; Or, the Rape Play started out as a reaction to the kind of nasty, misogynistic plays that have been adored by the masses for the past decade. But then it turned into an investigation of why we—meaning I—find this work compelling and repulsive at the same time. It attempts to critique the images while simultaneously trafficking in them. I don't believe it's right to blame the media for our objectification of women and/or the glamorization of heinous acts against them, because on some level we participate by going along for the ride. So this piece comes out of a deep ambivalence for the position we have put ourselves in as a society, with an eye toward its absurdity.

At the heart of these plays are some serious matters, but I am such an insecure person that I need to hear guffaws every few minutes or I feel like I'm suffocating. So, these plays attempt to pull humor from the morass—which is a bit like discovering one good tooth inside a mouth filled with rotten ones, then yanking it out by its roots and shouting, "Look what I found!" Laughter through the bleeding, that's what I'm after.

This might be one answer to a question I get asked constantly: "Why do you write plays?" It's an infuriatingly broad question— What is *really* being asked? Is it "why bother," which intimates that theater is a dying art? I don't agree—but that's a topic for another collection. Another answer is, "Because I *must*. A yawping, bottomless cavern in my soul compels me thusly." Which is true, kinda.

But for today, for this preface, my answer is that I'm waiting for someone to tell me to stop. And when they do, I'll make a deeply rude gesture with a few of my fingers. And then I'll scurry into a dark corner of my apartment in my pajamas, drink about seven cups of black Stumptown, crack open my MacBook, and pound out a freaky little number about a small woman in pajamas clawing the flesh off her palms to avoid boring herself.

Sheila Callaghan
Fall 2010

LASCIVIOUS
SOMETHING

★

ROADKILL
CONFIDENTIAL

★

THAT PRETTY
PRETTY;
OR,
THE RAPE
PLAY

LASCIVIOUS
SOMETHING

PRODUCTION HISTORY

Lascivious Something had its first official production on March 26, 2010, at Circle X Theatre Company in Los Angeles. Producer: Tim Wright. Director: Paul Willis. Assistant director: Lisa Szolovit. Set design: Sibyl Wickersheimer. Costume design: Dianne K. Graebner. Light design: Tom Ontiveros. Sound design: John Zalewski. Props: Ali Hisserich. Stage manager: Tina Baldwin. Assistant stage manager: Jessica M. Amezcua. Publicity: Lucy Pollak.

AUGUST	Silas Weir Mitchell
LIZA	Alina Phelan
BOY	Alana Dietze
DAPHNE	Olivia Henry

Lascivious Something had its Off-Broadway premiere on May 2, 2010, at the Julia Miles Theater in New York City, in a production by the Women's Project in association with Cherry Lane Theatre. Director: Daniella Topol. Set design: Marsha Ginsberg. Costume design: Theresa Squire. Lighting design: Chris Akerlind. Sound design: Broken Chord Collective. Production stage manager: Jack Gianino. Stage manager: Deanna Weiner. Production manager: Aduro Productions.

AUGUST	Rob Campbell
LIZA	Dana Eskelson
BOY	Ronete Levenson
DAPHNE	Elisabeth Waterston

CHARACTERS

AUGUST   male, late thirties
LIZA   female, late thirties
BOY   female, teenager
DAPHNE   female, twenty-four

SETTING

A remote Greek island.

TIME

1980.

NOTE

A stroke (/) marks the point of interruption in overlapping dialogue. When the stroke is not immediately followed by text, the next line should occur on the last syllable of the word before the slash—not an overlap but a concise interruption.

ACT ONE

AUGUST is weathered, emaciated, older than his age. He's covered in dirt and his fingers are stained red and covered in small cuts.

He is out in the field, tending his vines.

It is 1980.

AUGUST

My one hand. This hand, with its million minor cuts. Watched it move through the air. Watched it stretch its fingers toward the neck. The middle one trembling like a thin live wire. Curling as they reached the neck, curling around the back, finger finger finger finger thumb, then TOUCH, cool, like everything good in life, you know that kind of cool, and the red inside . . . the word I want to use is LUSH, red lush like the million minor cuts on my hands . . . but cooler than blood . . .

I knew then my life was about to change.

I held it by its neck, I felt its cool. I wondered if my blood would cool with it. I wondered if it could sense my touch somehow, if the atoms spun differently beneath my palm. I stood a respectful distance from it. Gripping. Not gripping, something more respectful than gripping. Because *I* was the one being gripped, you see. So. *Holding*, and I let the air between us fill and fill, with. With. That emotion you reserve only for the most holy of objects.

Brought it upstairs, placing both feet on each step, and allowed it to be taken from my hands just long enough to be placed into my carrier. How much, I heard myself asking. My heart did not race as I thought it would, but I did bite my tongue.

I barely saw the money leaving my fist, damp cash, barely saw the roiling concern in their eyes—they saw my cuts, I suppose, or maybe the worn soles of my sandals—and when the carrier was handed back to me its weight was sweeter than any weight that had ever loaded my pockets.

At home . . . You did WHAT, she said . . . but I hardly heard her. She was a little naked brown bean on the white sheets while I was plaster and roof and sky and clouds and black space. You did WHAT she said again, but with less conviction . . . and I realized she was making herself okay with it . . . The money. Everything.

And then she said. In her smallest, warmest voice. I hope you know what you're doing.

> *He regards the bottle and smiles widely.*

AUGUST *(cont.)*
A fundamental impossibility. Fuck yeah.

> DAPHNE *is seated at a worktable on a porch. She is twenty-four and poised, striking: a dark flower with a long willowy stem. She wears a work shirt and jeans.*
>
> *A modest, aging home sits behind her. She is surrounded by a trellis with grape leaves and bunches of fruit hanging down. September in the Mediterranean.*
>
> *She is scraping into a clay block. Every now and then she will consult a photo of the property.*
>
> LIZA *appears. She is weathered beyond her years, out of breath. She carries a small book and a small bag and wears a large-brimmed hat.*

LIZA
H-hello, I.

DAPHNE looks up and smiles. LIZA flips through her phrase book.

LIZA *(cont.)*
Sorry, *Ya-mas, Keery Moo. / Eethen*

DAPHNE *(Greek accent)*
I speak your language.

LIZA *(out of breath)*
Oh, super. There's a. Sign actually. TWO signs, but. A man with a donkey. Could I sit?

DAPHNE
Please.

LIZA
Thanks. I'm so winded! Kept thinking I was at the. Summit but then there'd be ANOTHER . . . so and gosh the donkey had like a beard?

DAPHNE
Ah.

LIZA
So I started up the. Thing again, but the path is all overgrown.

DAPHNE
My husband has been very busy. He means to cut down the wild grasses but it is harvest and we have only one boy full-time.

LIZA
Do you know the donkey I'm talking about?

DAPHNE
You are American?

LIZA
I am. It had a beard. And eyebrows.

DAPHNE

My husband is American. He does not see Americans often. We get British, Germans. Mostly the summer.

LIZA

And the fella was SUCH an excuse me asshole. I think he hates your. I don't know what he hates exactly.

DAPHNE

You say that why?

LIZA

He kept spitting. *Ftou, ftou!* Greek-greek-greek, *ftou!*

DAPHNE

He is short and like a prune.

LIZA

Prunelike, yes, and. Wheew. Angry?

DAPHNE

My husband will come up for his omelet shortly. Will you have some omelet with him?

LIZA

Um. Sure.

DAPHNE

You have arrived on a special day. It is the last day of harvest for the season.

LIZA

Hey! Great!

DAPHNE

How long do you anticipate staying with us?

LIZA

Hadn't figured / actually.

DAPHNE

We charge ten American dollars per night, or we have a weekly rate of sixty American dollars.

LIZA

Okay.

> DAPHNE *stands and retrieves a decanter filled with wine from the corner. She hands* LIZA *a glass and fills it.*

DAPHNE

Welcome to our island.

LIZA

Oh, it's . . . kind of early but what the heck! I'm on VACATION. Salut.

> LIZA *raises her glass.*

LIZA *(cont.)*

You aren't having any?

DAPHNE

No.

LIZA

Okay . . .

> LIZA *drinks deeply from the glass.* DAPHNE *returns to her scraping.*

LIZA *(cont.)*

SWEET.

DAPHNE

It is not good. It is the runoff, so it is fortunate you do not pay so much attention in the sipping.

LIZA

Oh. I never really do. Just sorta knock it back and wait to get. Heh dizzy.

DAPHNE *smiles politely.*

LIZA *(cont.)*
Boy, you're. Beautiful, I wasn't quite uh prepared . . .

DAPHNE
Where did you say you heard of us?

LIZA
This hostel in Italy, in Rome actually, and the—I've been traveling, so . . . and you know there's, they have the the. Corkboards. For backpackers.

DAPHNE
You do not have a backpack.

LIZA
No. Are you from nearby, or?

DAPHNE
My family is a small village a few kilometers away. *From*, is *from.* There are legends here . . . perhaps you shall hear some.

> LIZA *glances around the space and notices a black-and-white photograph.*

LIZA
Is this your . . .

DAPHNE
My husband, yes. Seven years ago.

LIZA
Nice. You took this?

DAPHNE
It was my semester abroad. I studied art. My thesis was a photo essay on the vineyards of the Napa Valley. Months later I brought him here.

LIZA
Why?

A beat.

DAPHNE
It's my family's land.

LIZA *examines the photo.*

LIZA
What's wrong with his eyes?

DAPHNE *takes the photo from* LIZA.

DAPHNE
It was harvest and he was an apprentice. Picking and pressing and tasting and not sleeping, he was drunk all the time . . . a piece of twine being frayed very slowly. (*A beat.*) He believes he is about to revolutionize the entire industry of winemaking. He does nothing small.

LIZA *looks up at the grapevines woven overhead.*

LIZA
Well I am delighted to be here. To be here in this place, this. Donkeys that need a shave, ha! And such a, an astonishing . . . It's. You know? HUMBLING. And these, these handsome . . .

DAPHNE
Help yourself.

LIZA
Don't you need them?

DAPHNE
We do not harvest those. They are for decoration. Please.

LIZA
Oh no no no no no . . .

DAPHNE *stands and picks a stem of grapes. She feeds one to* LIZA, *slowly.*

DAPHNE
You will find we are very generous people. Do not hesitate to ask for anything.

LIZA
. . . what's your name?

DAPHNE *(voiced TH, "Thahf'-nee")*
Daphne.

LIZA
Th. Oh, DAF-nee. Like in Scooby-Doo.

DAPHNE *(smiles)*
No. And how do they call you?

A *small beat.*

LIZA
Liza.

DAPHNE *maybe registers this.* LIZA *shoves the remainder of the grapes into her mouth.*

A *beat.*

LIZA *(cont.)*
As in "Minnelli." (*A beat.*) Is there somewhere I could go get cleaned / up?

DAPHNE
Of course. The guesthouse is down those steps and around the back. You are the first door, the suite. The key is in the handle and the sheets are starched and folded for the bed.

LIZA
Super. Thanks.

LIZA *exits.*

A beat. DAPHNE *realizes she is still holding the photo of* AUGUST. *She places it back on the table.*

AUGUST *sweeps into sight, singing loudly in Greek. He's a little tipsy.*

AUGUST
Na ena karidi
Na ena zoozooni
Fa'eh toh zoozooni prota
Ella hondreh'
(Here's a walnut
Here's a bug
Eat the bug first
Hey fatty)

He suddenly roars loudly.

AUGUST *(cont.)*
Aftos ine o thorivos pou kratousa mesa mou gia dio meres. (That is the sound I have been holding in for two days.)

DAPHNE
Sigharitiria, agapi mou. (Congratulations, my love.)

AUGUST
Thank you, *kota. Ine i sampania kria?* (Is the champagne chilled?)

DAPHNE
Ke pote den ine. (When is it not.)

AUGUST *retrieves a bottle from the cooler and pours himself a glass. She watches him carefully.*

DAPHNE *(cont.)*
Ehis homa sta hili sou. Pali tros homa . . . (You have earth on your lip. Eating your dirt again . . .)

AUGUST
Matheno pos i gevsi pezi mesa sta stafilia. Kita gia ton eafto sou. (I can taste how it plays into the grapes. See for yourself.)

He kisses her.

DAPHNE
Ick.

AUGUST
De tha fas homa. Woman. *Epidi ise homa.* (You won't eat dirt.
Woman. Because you ARE dirt.) Filthy filthy chicken . . .

He begins to kiss her. She notices his hands covered in cuts.

DAPHNE
Vlepis! Ti krima! (Look! What a pity!)

AUGUST
Ah, scissors broke again. Some reason the stems were so tough this
year . . .

DAPHNE *retrieves a damp rag.*

DAPHNE
Did Boy throw up?

AUGUST
You should see him down there with the crushers, pressing his
little heart out . . .

DAPHNE
Afto simeni ne? (That is yes?)

AUGUST
Yes. He threw up. At around five-thirty.

DAPHNE
Pini para poli sti sigomidi. (He drinks too much during harvest.)

AUGUST
Let him drink as much as he wants, long as it doesn't affect his
work . . .

DAPHNE

Ase to katharizma gia avrio. Ine methismenos / simera. (Save cleanup for tomorrow. He will be too hungover / today.)

AUGUST

He'll do as he's done every other year.

> *He touches her tummy.*

AUGUST *(cont.)*

Pos estanese? (How are you feeling?)

DAPHNE

Kourasmeni. I naftia me ksipnise. (Tired. The queasy woke me.)
He kisses her, then grabs a rag and begins wiping his hands.

AUGUST

You know what I was thinking today? How this all suddenly has a purpose. I mean it did before, but. I dunno. This little blastocyst . . . he's like a, like a root. Connecting us. I get all choked up thinking about it.

DAPHNE

Avgusto—

AUGUST

Ow. Weird. My knuckle. When I move my hand like this, my knuckle hurts. See like this, it hurts. Like this, it doesn't. This, ow. This, no. Ow, no. Ow, no.

DAPHNE

Kapios ine 'tho. (Someone is here.)

AUGUST

Here? From the village?

DAPHNE

Mia Americaneetha. (An American.)

AUGUST

That's odd . . . a tourist?

DAPHNE
Someone from your past. (*A beat.*) A woman.

AUGUST
Who?

> DAPHNE *does not answer.*

AUGUST *(cont.)*
Daphne . . .

DAPHNE
The one who bites.

> LIZA *enters.*

LIZA
I had trouble finding the . . .

> *She notices* AUGUST.

LIZA *(cont.)*
. . . bathroom.

AUGUST
Holy shit.

LIZA
Hello, August.

AUGUST
Holy shit. It's you. Is it you?

LIZA
It's me.

AUGUST
Ho. Lee. SHIT. What the hell are you doing here?

LIZA
I was just telling your your / wife

DAPHNE
I will go make the omelet. Excuse me.

> DAPHNE *exits.*

LIZA
I was telling . . . she is STUNNING, by the way.

AUGUST
Thank you.

LIZA
And so YOUNG.

AUGUST
Thank you . . . Liza! Wha . . .

LIZA
I was in Rome, and Romania, and Prague, and Buda-pescht /

> AUGUST *and* LIZA *begin kissing almost accidentally. Then*
> *they stop, embarrassed, surprised. Awkward.*

> DAPHNE *enters.*

DAPHNE
You might like to know, they said on the radio. Your president has
been elected. He is named Ronald Reagan.

> LIZA *exits.* AUGUST *and* DAPHNE *move into similar*
> *positions as those they were in before* LIZA *entered.*

AUGUST
Who?

> DAPHNE *does not answer.*

AUGUST *(cont.)*
Daphne . . .

DAPHNE
The one who bites.

LIZA *enters.*

LIZA
I had trouble finding the . . .

She notices AUGUST.

LIZA *(cont.)*
. . . bathroom.

AUGUST
Holy shit.

LIZA
Hello, August.

AUGUST
Holy shit. It's you. Is it you?

LIZA
It's me.

AUGUST
Ho. Lee. SHIT. What the hell are you doing here?

LIZA
I was just telling your your / wife

DAPHNE
I will go make the omelet. Excuse me.

DAPHNE *exits.*

LIZA
I was telling . . . she is STUNNING, by the way.

AUGUST
Thank you.

LIZA
And so YOUNG.

AUGUST

Thank you . . . Liza! Wha . . .

LIZA

I was in Rome, and Romania, and Prague, and Buda-pescht— (*A beat.*) Did you know that's how they pronounce it? With a "sht"?

AUGUST

I'm, I'm literally.

LIZA

PESSHHHT. I was doing some traveling, so . . . did you know Hungary has the highest, the highest um suicide rate of any other country? In the world?

AUGUST

You're a woman.

LIZA

Ha! I suppose I am.

AUGUST

You dropped all the baby fat.

LIZA

Ha! Well it was more like standard Grade D American Chub . . . Big Mac and a vanilla McShake every McFrickin' meal . . .

AUGUST

Are you hungry? Can I get you anything? Champagne?

> *He dashes over to the champagne bucket.*

LIZA

Strange we didn't see the irony of keeping our enemies in business . . . thanks . . . How is it that you look exactly the same?

AUGUST

I don't.

LIZA
You're swarthier, actually . . .

AUGUST
Swarthier? No.

LIZA
Not a little swarthier? Not even a little?

AUGUST
Knobbier, maybe. Less hair.

> *He hands her a glass of champagne, then realizes she still has her wine.*

AUGUST *(cont.)*
Oh, sorry, I didn't / even realize.

LIZA
No, it's, hang on . . .

> LIZA *downs her glass quickly.* AUGUST *is amused.*

AUGUST
You aren't a wine drinker.

LIZA
I'm no I don't suppose I mean a glass with dinner sometimes but.

AUGUST *(mischievous)*
Perfect. Are you as CLEVER as you ever were, Miss Liza?

LIZA
Clever-er, actually.

AUGUST
Then you shall learn. About such things. At this place. Are you as self-absorbed?

LIZA
You can't tell?

AUGUST
Then you will learn a lot, for fear of being made a fool.

LIZA
Ah. Well good.

AUGUST
Last question.

LIZA
Games, little August and his little / games.

AUGUST
Are you still a raging lunatic?

LIZA
Well of course. It's in my nature.

> AUGUST *hands her a glass of champagne.*

AUGUST
Then. Cheers.

> DAPHNE *enters with a large plate of eggs and three forks.*

> AUGUST *immediately begins wolfing it down.*

DAPHNE
I make it like the French. With heavy cream. An old French lesbian showed me how. She said Americans don't eat eggs. She said Americans therefore are the dangerous people. She had chickens in her back.

AUGUST
Back*yard.* She didn't have chickens in her. Heh.

DAPHNE
Her eggs came to the kitchen still warm from the chickens' bodies. Once we found a beak in the egg. A little baby beak.

AUGUST
Daphne's family spent their summers at various chateaux in Normandy. LOADED . . .

DAPHNE *offers a fork to* LIZA.

LIZA
Thank you.

LIZA *eats a forkful.*

DAPHNE
My lesbian also told me it is customary to spit into the eggs of our enemies.

LIZA *stops chewing.*

DAPHNE *(cont.)*
Fortunately, I do not spit. Spitting is a dirt habit. For people who eat dirt. You agree?

AUGUST
Talking about spitting while one is eating is also a dirt habit, *mikri-kota-mou.*

DAPHNE
Only from those with the dirt-mouth. You are not eating, Liza.

LIZA
I'd like to be drunk first, thanks. Great eggs.

DAPHNE
Thank you. You might like to know, they said on the radio. Your president has been elected. He is named Ronald Reagan. (*A slight beat, a slight smile.*) The actor.

LIZA *and* AUGUST *look at each other.* AUGUST *drinks.*

LIZA
I didn't realize you folks got American news over here.

DAPHNE
We receive the large news, the head—headlines, of course. We once received American newspapers to the house. But then I

stopped allowing them. You know that vine in his neck, the big vine? When he would read the American news his vine would pop.

LIZA

Vein, I think. Right?

DAPHNE

He has a grapevine in his neck. Tell her, *Avgusto*.

AUGUST

I have a grapevine in my neck, Liza. It used to be a vein. But now when I bleed. My blood is wine. Delicious eggs, my filthy chicken. You know, tonight? We should have a feast. For Liza.

DAPHNE

Of course we should.

LIZA

Oh, no . . .

AUGUST

What do you eat?

LIZA

Don't go to any. I wasn't even planning on / staying.

AUGUST

There are no other guesthouses for miles.

LIZA

I eat everything.

AUGUST

A feast then. For the last day of harvest AND for a long lost friend. More champagne?

LIZA

No thank you. All right.

> *He pours.*

DAPHNE

Liza! You are the first old friend of my husband's which whom I have met. I would very much like to hear a story from his youth.

LIZA

A story? Like what kind of . . .

DAPHNE

A badly behaved story. I'm sure he has many.

LIZA

Um . . . I met him senior year of high school, so . . . he was a, oh God a WRETCHED student. I mean he was a genius, but. But he liked to do, heh. Bad things. To teachers. Like have AFFAIRS with them.

AUGUST

Ha! I forgot about that!

LIZA

Oh please, how could you / have POSSIBLY.

DAPHNE

Affairs. Love affairs.

AUGUST

Man oh / man . . .

DAPHNE

I am not shocked.

AUGUST

Just the one, Liza is hyperbolizing /

LIZA

One was / PLENNY

DAPHNE

I don't know that word, / Hyper . . .

LIZA

She was so OLD!

AUGUST

No she was / not.

LIZA

She was what, fifty, / fifty-five?

AUGUST

THIRTY-five. Ish.

DAPHNE

You were how / old?

AUGUST

I don't / recall.

LIZA

Seventeen. He got EXPELLED. For BONING his chemistry teacher! She was, is, is this an appropriate / story?

AUGUST

It's fine.

DAPHNE

Go on.

LIZA

Well he was planning on dropping out anyway. Was on this angsty kick against formal education.

AUGUST

Heh /

LIZA

Wanted to eat garbage and write leftist propaganda. They called him "Mega-Marx"!

AUGUST

You're leaving out the best part of the story!

LIZA

Oh! So this teacher wasn't just ANY teacher . . . she was BLACK. A BLACK teacher in a white public school system. In suburban New Jersey. In 1963. You can just imagine the uproar from the—do, do you know anything about the American Civil Rights movement?

DAPHNE

Yes.

LIZA

Well anyway. She got very fired AND very publicly ostracized . . . And a week later, he showed up to the Board of Ed meeting with about twenty angry teenagers. All in blackface.

      AUGUST *and* LIZA *laugh.*

DAPHNE

Ha. That is an amusing. I also know a story. It is one involving you.

LIZA

Really? What?

DAPHNE

I'm sure if you thought hard you would think it up.

LIZA

I am thinking hard . . .

AUGUST

Miss Liza, what is the one story my wife would have to know?

LIZA

I really can't imagine . . .

      AUGUST *stands and turns his body to the side, and pulls*
      down his pants. A puffy, bite-shaped scar is dug into his hip.

DAPHNE

You and he were living out of your small car at the San Francisco Bay. You had no more food. You had not washed yourselves in two weeks besides your feet in the water. You had sex four times a day and were on pot much of the time. You were lying with your stringy head in his lap with your eyes closed. You were talking about molecules moving in your fingers and your feet. You were talking about how your skin was not solid, how the vinyl seat was not solid. You said everything was vibrating in nature at all times, and you said it scared you so much, and you said the only time you felt still was when his voice was in your ears, low and serious. And then you felt a wet drop on your closed lids, and you opened them and he was crying into your eyes. And he said you are so beautiful Liza, you are so beautiful you could crack the sky open. And you said August you are like the universe, you are so big you fill me you fill my ears and you fill me. He brought his head down to yours and unrolled his tongue into your mouth. And his fingers wound around your hair. And you grabbed his hip with your hand and you said the word NEED, and you wrapped your thick leg around his skinny leg and said the word NEED, and then you sank your teeth into his hip and bit so hard you came back with part of him in your mouth. And then you made love. And you fell asleep. And when you woke up you had a red smear on your face where you fell asleep in his blood. But he was gone. (*A beat.*) That was the last time you saw him.

LIZA
Huh. I don't remember that.

AUGUST
You do, Liza.

LIZA
I don't, really. Biting. I'd remember a thing like that. But I do have the urge quite often. To bite people. I just don't think I'd follow it through.

AUGUST
Of course you would. You want to bite my wife right now. Admit it.

LIZA
Ha! Sure! I'll bite her face off!

AUGUST
I think you just might.

LIZA
What? Shut up.

DAPHNE
She will. She is about to.

LIZA
Bite your face? No, honey. I will not bite your face.

AUGUST
Do it. Go on. Bite her.

DAPHNE
August—

> *A long beat.* LIZA *looks as though she might bite* DAPHNE's *face. She does. Chaos. Then . . .*

DAPHNE *(cont.)*
Ha. That is an amusing. I also know a story. It is one involving you.

LIZA
Really? What?

DAPHNE
I'm sure if you thought hard you would think it up.

LIZA
I am thinking hard . . .

AUGUST
Miss Liza, what is the one story my wife would have to know?

LIZA
I really can't imagine . . .

> AUGUST *stands and digs into his pocket, and takes out a package of Wint-o-Green Life Savers.*

LIZA *(cont.)*
Oh NO!!

> *He pops three in his mouth and begins to chew, smiling hugely.*
> LIZA *begins cracking up.*

DAPHNE
He is obsessed. Impossible to get over here, I have / them shipped.

LIZA
You told her!

AUGUST
No choice, I'm / afraid.

DAPHNE
He tells me everything.

LIZA
Roll after roll, / the whole trip . . .

AUGUST
Ha ha!

LIZA
Getting high in our car every night, reading passages from Reagan's autobiography—

AUGUST
It had a great title, didn't it, a line in a movie where he played an amputee . . . um . . . *Where's the Rest of Me? The Ronald Reagan Story.*

DAPHNE
What / ah . . .

LIZA
That's it! And THEN, we'd turn off our flashlights and you'd haul out the Wint-o-Greens . . .

AUGUST
Fireworks!! Every time!! God that was . . . it was epic. Wasn't it?

LIZA
It was. And you had like a theory, a real scientific THING / for the whole.

AUGUST
Not theory. Fact. All hard sugar-based candies emit some degree of light when you bite them. It's called um triboluminescence.

DAPHNE
I don't know that / word.

AUGUST
The emission of light resulting from something being smashed or, or / torn.

LIZA
You ass. It's MAGIC. A little electrical storm in your mouth.

AUGUST
But well YES. That's exactly what it is.

DAPHNE
Don't think me rude for saying this but I feel as though you should not be calling my husband a donkey. Thank you. Pardon me . . . (*Begins cleaning up the dishes.*) "Boning." This means to make love.

AUGUST
. . . yes.

DAPHNE
I was not certain.

> DAPHNE *exits. A beat.*

AUGUST
Well.

LIZA
Well.

> *A small beat.*

AUGUST
Fucking Reagan—

LIZA
I KNOW! I mean he was way ahead in the polls this week, but I thought maybe, just maybe . . . I mean not really but.

AUGUST
Were you in on any of that?

LIZA
I tried, man. We were going door to door right up until I got on the plane.

AUGUST
Not for Carter?

LIZA
God no. Voter registration. I work for the ACLU. We focus on former convicts, the disenfranchised, et cetera.

AUGUST *(impressed)*
Pounding the pavement for / the people's rights . . .

LIZA
Well mostly I'm behind a desk in a tiny gray office drinking bad coffee and working for pennies. But yeah.

AUGUST
Where?

LIZA
Berkeley.

AUGUST
Still?

LIZA
Jealous?

AUGUST

I am. We had quite a little thing going, didn't we. Sweating into our Keds outside / the Safeway . . .

LIZA

The Safeway, yeah.

AUGUST

. . . looting AV equipment from the student union . . .

LIZA

We kept at it after you left. Got pretty close. We were only about two hundred thousand signatures away from qualifying for the ballot to kick Reagan out of the governor's office . . .

AUGUST

Wow. That's—

LIZA

Fat lotta good it did.

AUGUST

Still. You tried.

    A small beat.

LIZA

We fell apart two weeks later. We needed you man. Everyone wanted to know where you had gone. I told them Canada. Said you'd be back when the draft was over. I went looking, once . . . Mendecino, Humbolt, Crescent City even . . . Not even a postcard. (*A beat.*) You gonna tell me what happened?

AUGUST (*with difficulty*)

Yeah, okay. I was making this speech one day—it was a Thursday, that's when I had the morning shift at the Copymat—so I had this stack of stolen flyers, and I was screaming about how everyone should hurl their bodies onto the gears of the machine, right . . . but for some reason I started getting panicky . . . then I was floating above myself, looking down at the throngs of kids . . . and suddenly it was like *I was* the machine . . . So I just, I fucking lost it. Grabbed the stack of flyers and chucked them at the crowd. Left town the next day.

A beat.

LIZA
I'm sorry.

AUGUST
You couldn't have done anything. Some people were meant for greatness. I'm not one of them.

A long beat. AUGUST *drinks.*

LIZA *(trying)*
But . . . you're doing something here, right? Something big? With your vineyard? Your wife said—

AUGUST
I'm trying . . .

LIZA
She said you're revolutionizing the wine industry.

AUGUST
I'm *trying.* I planted a rare varietal.

LIZA
What's that?

AUGUST
A derivation of a common regional grape called *mavrodaphne.* Traditionally it is a sweet communion wine, but I vinified a DRY *mavrodaphne.* This country has no wine trade, so if it takes off . . . well the economy here could use it . . . and we'd have a cheap decent bottle for the locals, so . . . That's something. Right?

LIZA
Hell yeah. That's fucking amazing!

AUGUST
You think?

LIZA
Yeah! It's great, August. You—you have this—eating the world with your eyes kind of thing . . .

> DAPHNE *emerges. She is dressed differently, more elegantly, but still appropriately, possibly in a flowered dress. She is now wearing makeup. She carries freshly cut flowers. They are odd and wild and beautiful.*

DAPHNE
I feel better now. It is a superb weather today. This year's harvest will be extraordinary, with this orange sun and thickly spiced air . . .

AUGUST
Did Daphne show you the label? Show her, *kota* . . .

> DAPHNE *retrieves a print from her work area. She shows* LIZA.

DAPHNE
It is not done . . . you see I need to fill in the details on the leaves. Also the wood grain on the barrels.

> LIZA *examines the print.*

LIZA
I like it.

DAPHNE
Avgusto does not.

AUGUST
I love it. It's just, it's a little. Stately, but.

DAPHNE
He wants it to have more whimsy and wickedness.

AUGUST
It's beautiful.

LIZA

Where's the, the thingie? The title.

DAPHNE

The name is secret. He will not tell even me. I think he does not have one.

AUGUST

Oh, I have a name. It is top secret. I want to taste it first before I make it official.

LIZA

You haven't tasted it?

AUGUST

I'm superstitious. Two more days, Liza. I feel like a little kid. Will you still be here?

LIZA

Do you want me to be?

AUGUST

Of course, yes, I would very much like you to stay for it.

LIZA

Would you.

AUGUST

I . . . ha.

LIZA

Could you tell me where the bathroom is?

AUGUST

Through the kitchen and down the uh, the stairs.

LIZA

Thank you. Whoo. I'm a little. Tipsy, actually I might like to nap. I didn't sleep much on the. Boat, a baby kept crying . . .

DAPHNE
Of course. I will come down with a glass of water for you shortly.

LIZA
No need . . .

DAPHNE
Very well. Shall you have a legend when you come back?

LIZA
That's /okay.

DAPHNE
Has she earned a legend, *Avgusto?*

AUGUST *(playful)*
Indeed. She's earned two.

LIZA
Swell. See you in a while.

AUGUST
Sleep well . . .

> *She exits.* AUGUST *and* DAPHNE *are tense around each other a moment.*

DAPHNE
Thelo na sou 'po, then nomizo oti prepi na ine 'tho / avrio yia toh—
(I have to say, I don't think she should be here tomorrow for the—)

AUGUST
English, *kota*, I'm too tired to translate . . .

DAPHNE
Uurrg. I am weary of English. It is such a pointy language. Many corners and very little curves. I feel when I speak it I am walking around a small room with large pieces of sharp furniture.

AUGUST
It's good practice. You're out of practice.

DAPHNE

I also feel this way around your friend . . . (*A beat.*) You told me she was dead.

AUGUST

I said she was *probably* dead.

DAPHNE

Why do you imagine she's here?

AUGUST

She's traveling . . .

DAPHNE

It is not usual.

AUGUST

She saw a posting. We're in that book; they all have the same guidebook.

DAPHNE

Will she be paying?

AUGUST

She's our guest, Daphne.

DAPHNE

She was not invited. We need the money. I cannot bear to go to my father again. Not after last time.

AUGUST

I'll ask her to leave. Would you like that?

DAPHNE

I do not think she should be here for the tasting.

AUGUST

Why not?

DAPHNE

It is an intimate moment. You do not know what to expect. It could be a triumph but also it could be a disappointment—

LIZA *reappears.*

LIZA
Sorry. There's a girl in the bed.

DAPHNE
That is Boy. He is passed out. Just move him gently to one side.

LIZA
Oh. Okay.

LIZA *disappears. A beat.*

AUGUST
I'll tell her we need the rooms. Or that you aren't up to entertaining. I'll think of something.

DAPHNE *begins scraping into her block in agitation.*

AUGUST *(cont.)*
She was never good around other women. Didn't have many girlfriends. Hid in corners, that sort of. People thought she was mental. Got into fights a lot, this thing she'd do . . . I thought it was funny at the time. She'd bring a, a pair of scissors to class and snip the hair of whoever sat in front of her.

DAPHNE
Oh. I like that.

AUGUST
You would have been the girl whose hair was snipped.

DAPHNE
Do not be ridiculous. I commanded respect at that age. I had many friends, even the ugly girls. They threw a party of me at fifteen. It was a surprise. I remember I had stolen a dress that day. Did I tell you about this?

AUGUST
No.

DAPHNE

I stole a designer dress from the department store. I could have bought it myself. I had the money . . . It was a very pretty dress. It had sparkle, you know? Those bits that catch the light. Not diamonds, the other word. But I didn't want it badly enough to pay. And it was my birthday. I thought if I got caught I would tell the men it is my birthday, and they would let me take it anyway. But I did not get caught. In the room where you try things on, I put on the dress, then I put on my longer dress over it, and then I walked home. And my heart was so light. And I arrived home and my house was full of my friends, all smiling and eating little foods on plates. And there was a pile of *cadeaux* in the corner, eh, gifts. And I took off my long dress and beneath I was sparkling, and everyone shouted "Ahhh!" and applauded. As if I could have known I had a party waiting for me. It was luck! I've always been lucky like that.

AUGUST

I bet you were beautiful.

DAPHNE

I could sparkle for you now, if you like. I will become a holiday. I will decorate myself with twinkle lights and sing a song about a man who buries his heart in the dirt and later eats the dirt to remember how the heart tasted. (*A beat.*) I will behave myself around your *amour perdu* . . .

AUGUST

You're fine.

> DAPHNE *begins to Greek dance a little, her arms out.*
> AUGUST *watches her.*

DAPHNE

Look. Can you see them? My twinkle lights . . .

> DAPHNE *turns on the radio from before. She dances for him.*

> *He claps along halfheartedly. She pulls* AUGUST *from his seat.*

AUGUST
Too tired, *kota* . . .

DAPHNE
This will enervise you . . .

> AUGUST *begins dancing.* AUGUST*'s steps are clumsy.*

DAPHNE *(cont.)*
Your Greek dancing is appalling.

AUGUST
I'm not Greek.

DAPHNE
Can you not get your back any straighter?

AUGUST
It doesn't go any straighter.

DAPHNE
Of course it does.

> AUGUST *begins dancing absurdly.*

AUGUST
Opa!!

DAPHNE
Don't say that. You sound like an American.

AUGUST
Opa!! Opa!! Ella! Yia-sou!

> AUGUST *stops dancing.*

DAPHNE
An insult to my people . . .

AUGUST
I'll take lessons . . .

DAPHNE
You are beyond correction . . .

AUGUST
Find me a teacher.

>   *A small beat.*

DAPHNE *(melancholy, distant)*
There are no men in the village who would teach a husband of mine.

AUGUST
Don't think about that right now . . .

>   AUGUST *draws Daphne into him. They slow dance.*

DAPHNE
My father had a friend, and old man . . . at every wedding he would dance for hours. His jumps were so high. Balloon, they used to call him. You could not stop him. Not even to feed him. He is dead now . . .

AUGUST
Did he dance himself to death?

DAPHNE
Yes.

AUGUST *(stops dancing)*
Are you trying to kill me, *kota*?

DAPHNE
Yes.

AUGUST
But you aren't a dangerous woman. You are a brown bean.

DAPHNE
Would you like me to be dangerous? I could be.

AUGUST
No . . .

DAPHNE
I have a little danger in me. A very little.

AUGUST
I know where your danger is.

He touches her belly, then below.

DAPHNE
Yes . . .

AUGUST
Filthy . . . filthy . . .

DAPHNE
Ne . . .

They begin kissing passionately.

Lights down. They continue kissing as . . .

A radio broadcast is heard. Music, scratchy, news from America, spoken with an English accent.

ANNOUNCER (V.O.)
This is the BBC. Now your news from America. The former Hollywood actor and Republican governor of California Ronald Reagan is to be the next president of the United States. He has defeated Democrat Jimmy Carter in the U.S. presidential elections by a landslide. The last speech of Mr. Reagan's campaign was followed by a dazzling firework display, after which he returned to his home in Pacific Palisades to spend polling day resting.

During the next thirty years, certain sectors of the global economy will experience unprecedented levels of growth, due to Reagan's deregulatory approach. Many industries, including winemaking, will enjoy an unexpected boom. People will spend beyond their means, buy homes they cannot afford, borrow money from corrupt sources. But eventually, the bubble shall pop. This will of course result in a worldwide financial crisis. One of the casualties of this disaster will be Greece. (*A beat.*)

In other news . . . things often burst. They burst.

> *Lights up on the porch. It is eight hours later. The remains of a huge feast lie out on the table. Two empty bottles of wine and one half-empty bottle are on the table.*

> LIZA *sits at the table alone. She surveys the carnage of the meal and chomps Wint-o-Green after Wint-o-Green. She is distant, troubled.*

> BOY, *a teenage girl dressed as a boy in jeans and a cap, sneaks onto the porch. She is covered in soil and her fingertips are stained red. She walks sloppily and slouchy, all elbows and hips.*

> BOY *loads up a plate of food for herself. She then moves to the corner and eats in silence, taking occasional swigs from a bottle of half-drunk wine.*

> *A beat.*

LIZA
Do you live here?

> BOY *doesn't answer.*

LIZA *(cont.)*
Before . . . earlier, I mean, in the . . .

> BOY *doesn't answer.*

LIZA *(cont.)*
Do you speak? At all?

> BOY *guzzles her wine.*

LIZA *(cont.)*

Where are your parents?

> *DAPHNE enters.*

DAPHNE *(to LIZA)*

Kali spera. (Good evening.) Have you eaten enough?

LIZA

Um yeah. Enough for a week . . .

DAPHNE

I am sorry you did not come on our walk with us. The sun setting onto the hill is *poli orea.* Very beautiful.

LIZA

Sunset, Christ . . . we were eating three hours straight . . .

DAPHNE

Yes. We do this. Lengthy eating. It is fortunate I enjoy to cook. It calms me. Did you know in Greece we have eighty-six ways to say "stop feeding me"?

LIZA

Why does that not surprise me?

DAPHNE

I do not understand the question.

LIZA

No, it. I meant. That it doesn't surprise me.

DAPHNE

Are you not easily surprised?

LIZA

Actually. Everything surprises me.

DAPHNE

Do I surprise you?

LIZA
In what way?

DAPHNE
When you first appeared you said I was beautiful, and then you said you were not prepared. This reveals you had an expectation. "The wife of *Avgusto* will be unattractive."

LIZA *laughs.*

DAPHNE *(cont.)*
You laugh because it rings of truth.

LIZA
Well I suppose I "expected" him to be with a woman who was alive when Kennedy was shot.

DAPHNE
I was alive. I was seven.

LIZA
Right.

DAPHNE
Does the age difference affect you?

LIZA
I was kidding / around.

DAPHNE
American women are threatened by age. Why is this?

LIZA
Well, I don't know too many American women, so.

DAPHNE
No, I suppose you are uncommon. *Avgusto* would not care for a common woman. (*Smiles hugely.*) You see how I compliment you and turn it back around to me? That is a cultural thing. French, I mean. I identify often with the French. Greek women tend to

be more. There is an English word that means "under the service of men" . . .

LIZA
And you aren't?

DAPHNE
Of course I am. But it is different when the man is equally under the service of the woman. Yes?

LIZA
Ah. (*A beat. LIZA peers around.*) So is, is he . . .

DAPHNE
He will be up shortly. He said he has getting something special. *Is.*

LIZA
Not dessert I hope.

DAPHNE
He did not say.

>*An awkward silence.*

DAPHNE *(cont.)*
Tell me about where you live.

LIZA
I'd rather not.

DAPHNE
Why?

LIZA
I'm in transition.

DAPHNE
Surely you have a place to hang your clothing.

LIZA
I don't own a tremendous amount of clothing.

DAPHNE

You are being coy.

LIZA

No. I had, I DID have an apartment. In a building.

DAPHNE

A tall building? A "sky . . ." a sky /

LIZA

Not really. It, um. Six stories. Old carpet. The elevator is always broken. A radiator, um, you know don't take this the wrong way? I am not. Good at this. Aimless chatter. I kind of hate it.

DAPHNE

You are doing beautifully.

LIZA

I kind of really hate it. (*A beat.*) And now, you're. Um LOOKING at me, so, and I, I already talked about the food, and the view, the sunset, and I don't really want to talk about August, so. (*A beat.*) Is there more wine?

> DAPHNE *walks over to* BOY *and pries the bottle from her hands, pouring* LIZA *a glass. She returns the bottle to* BOY, *who continues to guzzle it.*

DAPHNE

Liza, I feel I must be frank to you. I do not trust you. BUT, it is one of the reasons I feel so compelled by you.

LIZA

Oh.

DAPHNE

And you both speak very fast around one another, which also makes me feel strange.

LIZA

It's chilly, isn't it?

DAPHNE

We are without friends here and I feel grateful for your company and therefore I feel generous toward you. I wonder if you would like Boy to help you with anything.

LIZA

No. Should she be / drink—

DAPHNE

He is fine.

LIZA

Can she, okay, *he* speak English?

DAPHNE

Only "how are you" and "have a nice day."

LIZA

He, actually she. Before, when I was sleeping.

DAPHNE

Yes. He likes to massage sometimes. Do not let it offend you. I wonder if it felt nice, though.

LIZA

Um.

DAPHNE

It is meant to relax you.

LIZA

Oh.

DAPHNE

I will mention to him not to do it again. But let us continue to talk frankly. I would like you to tell me something. With being frank.

LIZA

With being frank. Okay.

DAPHNE
Why are you here?

LIZA
That's a great question, Daphne. I'll answer it. Sure, no problem. I'll answer your question. I have no problem answering that question.

> *They stare each other down for several moments. It should be so long it looks as though both actors have forgotten their lines. REALLY long. No shorter than twenty seconds.*

DAPHNE
But let us continue to talk frankly. I would like you to tell me something. With being frank.

LIZA
With being frank. Okay.

DAPHNE
Why are you here?

LIZA
I have something belonging to August that I need to return.

> *A long beat.* DAPHNE *smiles.*

DAPHNE
I love the American sense of humor.

> LIZA *stares blankly at her.*
>
> *Some time passes where neither woman says a word.*

DAPHNE *(cont.)*
Perhaps you shall tell me later.

> AUGUST *is hooting off stage. He enters holding something in a bag very preciously.*

LIZA
Finally! What took you so long?

AUGUST

I was having a moment of. Of rapture, one could say? (*He places the bag gently onto the table.*) You missed a freakin' PHENOMENAL sunset, / Liza-Maria.

LIZA

I heard . . .

AUGUST

Haven't seen a sunset like that since our first harvest, remember Daphne?

DAPHNE

I / do.

AUGUST

The sky all bloody and diabolical . . . Christ I can't *wait* to taste it. Thirty-seven hours . . .

> AUGUST *notices* BOY *in the corner. She has passed out. He kicks at her feet.*

AUGUST *(cont.) (playful)*

Hey! Ine mono yia tous megaloos! Adults only! *Fee'yeh apo 'do.* (This is FOR ADULTS ONLY! Adults only. Get out of here.)

BOY

Ande gameesoo, ye-ro! (Fuck you old man!)

AUGUST *(amused)*

Ho! Did you hear that?

DAPHNE

The mouth on him!

AUGUST

Proxekse, ee tha reekso krio nero sta moo'tra soo san kee'mase . . . (Watch out, or I'll dump a cup of cold water on your head while you sleep . . .)

BOY

Eho panta ina matee anee'hto. Kai ime pyo gree'goros apo 'sena. (I sleep with one eye open. And I'm faster than you.)

> *They scuffle playfully.*

DAPHNE *(laughing)*
Be careful, you'll hurt him!

LIZA
Why do you keep doing that? Calling her a him?

AUGUST
Just a game . . .

> AUGUST *hands* BOY *the open bottle of wine.*

AUGUST *(cont.)*
Go on!

> BOY *exits.*

AUGUST *(cont.)*
Now. We have some veeeery important business to attend to. Ahem. Close your eyes, Liza.

DAPHNE
Thavmastiko! Ti Hara! (Wonderful! How fun!) This will be fun . . .

LIZA
W-what's / going on—

AUGUST
Close 'em!

LIZA
Jeez, okay!

> LIZA *closes her eyes. This is the ultimate game.*

AUGUST *(fun, painting a picture)*
Ready? Legend one. It is May 1906. We are in the southwest of France, the Médoc region. We are at a famous chateau, which

makes a very famous Bordeaux. It is a warm and rainy spring. Can you feel it?

LIZA
Definitely . . .

DAPHNE *(to LIZA)*
He loves telling this . . .

> *Throughout, it is* AUGUST *telling the story and* DAPHNE *making playful sound effects, helping to tell it. It is their story . . . until it becomes* LIZA's.

AUGUST
We are kneeling in a small, experimental patch of vines. We are a young man and a young woman. We are slowly taking off one another's clothes.

LIZA
Oooh! Which one am I?

AUGUST
Either, both. We do this every day, explore each other when we should be tending the vines. We cannot help ourselves.

LIZA
Mmmmm.

AUGUST
Our vineyard manager does not see us. He is more concerned with the main plots. But he is in love with one of us. Fiercely. There is history here.

LIZA
Racy!

AUGUST
Indeed! The spring months ripen into summer, and the world goes hot and dry. But we do not notice. And when our vines are attacked by deadly moths, we do not notice.

A beat.

But he does. He comes down the hill early one morning, and he sees . . . one hand in the other's hair, one hand in the other's mouth. He tears us apart and slaps one of us in the face, the one whom he loves. The unslapped one flees the vineyard in a hot wash of shame.

LIZA
Oh . . .

AUGUST
The slapped one remains, and must do the work of two, and quickly, as the moth infestation is spreading.

Then. Press press press, into the wire grid, press press fingers wrinkled and stained purple, press press press press press press press press press press press press . . .

The million minor cuts are the last things to touch these grapes. The grapes, conversely, are the last things to touch these young hands in this field during this hot dry September in 1906 . . . for late one evening, on the last day of harvest, the blade of the vine scissors will slice . . . Two. Young. Wrists.

LIZA
Jesus . . .

        AUGUST *pauses long.*

DAPHNE
Only twenty bottles were produced from this slim crop. And—

        AUGUST shuts DAPHNE down with a curt gesture and a
        sound.

AUGUST
Twenty bottles were produced. And they are legendary.

        DAPHNE *moves elsewhere to pout while he continues without her.*

        AUGUST *touches the wine holder.*

AUGUST *(cont.)*

Six of the bottles were lost in an estate fire in 1940. Three bottles were auctioned off to a Swiss heir in the thirties. A German wine collector boasts of owning five bottles himself. Three bottles are unaccounted for. Two bottles have been sampled at vertical tastings, one in sixty-four and one in seventy-three, and both times the wines were described as "astonishing."

> AUGUST *unsheathes the old, dusty bottle. It has a crusted yellowing etched label. He holds it sideways, presenting it.*

AUGUST *(cont.)*

And one of the bottles, Liza, is here.

> LIZA *opens her eyes . . . and sees the bottle . . . and gasps a little.*

AUGUST *(cont.)*

We spent every penny we had on this. It was worth twice that.

> *A long beat.*

LIZA

You're going to open it now, aren't you?

> AUGUST *takes a moment to decide. Then, he places the bottle upright.*

AUGUST

Blame the sunset. Blame the harvest.

LIZA *(electrified)*

Oh my God . . .

AUGUST

I always knew I'd *feel* when the right moment came along. And I swore to myself I would not let it pass. People do that, they. Second-guess themselves . . .

LIZA

But you never do, August.

AUGUST
No, Bitchadeeto. I do not.

LIZA
Oh my gosh oh my gosh . . .

> AUGUST *removes a bottle opener from his pocket.* DAPHNE *is stone.*

AUGUST
This probably won't work, the uh. Cork might be a little decrepit . . .

> AUGUST *places three huge-globed wine glasses on the table. He then retrieves a very long-necked glass decanter. He gestures to the candle.*

AUGUST
Light that.

> LIZA *lights the candle.*

> AUGUST *lines it up next to the neck of the bottle, peering at it through the glass. Then he wipes down the bottle with a cloth and very carefully removes the cork.*

AUGUST *(cont.)*
. . . got most of it . . .

> *He smells the cork, then wipes down the neck of the bottle again.*

LIZA
So exciting . . . my heart is pounding . . .

> AUGUST *places the decanter beneath the mouth of the bottle. He places both elbows on the table and very slowly, he begins to pour.*

> *The wine begins to flow steadily, slowly, along the side of the decanter.*

> *He watches the neck closely, lit by the candle.*

AUGUST

. . . no one make me laugh . . .

LIZA

What's the candle for?

AUGUST

To see the sediment at the shoulder . . . shhhh.

> *The decanter fills.*

AUGUST *(cont.)*

Daphne. Can you believe we're doing this?

DAPHNE

No.

AUGUST

. . . look at that color . . .

LIZA

Someone should take a picture . . .

> DAPHNE *retrieves her camera. She aims the lens at* LIZA.

LIZA *(cont.)*

Not, not me . . . him.

> DAPHNE *continues to focus on* LIZA.

LIZA *(cont.)*

HIM . . .

DAPHNE

I want to remember this moment. Every detail.

> LIZA *hides her face with her hair.* DAPHNE *takes the picture.*

AUGUST

. . . almost there . . .

DAPHNE *turns the camera on* AUGUST. *He smiles goofily. She snaps a picture.*

The decanter is full.

AUGUST *carefully pours wine into the three glasses.*

DAPHNE *takes another picture.*

AUGUST *(cont.)*
Okay. Ladies, retrieve your glasses. We are about to drink history.

LIZA *retrieves her glass.*

DAPHNE *very calmly places her camera on the table next to the wine.*

DAPHNE
Goodnight, *Avgusto.*

She exits.

AUGUST *and* LIZA *are silent a moment, holding their glasses.*

LIZA
Um, okay what . . . ?

AUGUST
Oh.

LIZA
. . . What . . .

AUGUST
Oh. Oh.

He sinks to the ground in misery.

LIZA
August . . .

AUGUST
I totally, I completely . . . she's pregnant.

> LIZA *begins to hyperventilate. She crushes the glass in her*
> *hand. Her fist explodes in wine.* AUGUST *does not notice.*
> LIZA *retrieves another glass.*

AUGUST *(cont.)*
She's pregnant.

LIZA
I really like this wi—

> LIZA *crushes another glass. She retrieves another.*

AUGUST
She's pregnant.

LIZA
But. She saw you take three glasses out, she didn't say anything . . .

AUGUST
I should have . . . You know? *Immediately.*

LIZA
Why didn't she SAY some / thing?

AUGUST
It's not her style. DAMN IT!

LIZA
Style? That's ridicu / lous.

AUGUST
Not everyone expresses everything.

LIZA
Maybe it's an age thing . . .

AUGUST
No. It's a *her* thing.

LIZA

Well. (*A long beat.*) You're uh . . . you're gonna make a great fuckin' dad. (*Another long beat.*) Aren't you, you're not gonna go down there / and try to?

AUGUST

No, no. She's otherwise occupied by now I'm sure.

LIZA

Oh. What does that / mean?

AUGUST

Nothing.

> *A beat.*

LIZA

So. Um what I'm holding in my hand? Is basically your life's savings.

AUGUST

Pretty much.

LIZA

Wonder if Karl Marx ever spent his life's savings on a bottle of wine . . .

AUGUST

Probably not.

> *A beat.*

LIZA

You aren't going to let it go to waste, are you?

> AUGUST *holds the glass up to the moon.*

AUGUST

Hold your glass up to the moon.

> LIZA *holds the glass up by the globe.*

AUGUST *(cont.)*
By the stem.

>   LIZA *switches her grip.*

AUGUST *(cont.)*
See how clear the moon is through the wine?

LIZA
Yeah.

AUGUST
That's a very very good sign.

LIZA
Of what?

AUGUST
That your mind is about to be blown.

LIZA
Okay.

AUGUST
Swirl it in your glass.

>   *She does. He does.*

AUGUST *(cont.)*
Now tip your nose in. Inhale.

>   *She does. He does.*

AUGUST *(cont.)*
Now take only a little . . . wash your entire mouth in it . . . feel it
on every bump on your tongue . . .

>   *She does. He does.*

AUGUST *(cont.)*
Oh . . . oh . . .

His eyes remain shut, his mouth working aggressively. He is tasting the hell out of the wine, for a really long time.

After a while . . .

AUGUST *(cont.)*
Just . . .

LIZA
Right?

AUGUST
I know.

LIZA
This.

AUGUST
I couldn't have even . . .

LIZA
. . . is a beverage . . .

He opens his eyes. They kiss sensuously.

A beat.

AUGUST
Thank you.

LIZA
No problem.

A beat.

AUGUST
You should . . . keep drinking, the uh. Because it's old, the longer it sits out and oxidizes the more its. Quality declines . . .

AUGUST *sips.*

LIZA
Night of a thousand legends.

AUGUST
Got any for me?

LIZA
One. But I might save it.

AUGUST
For a rainy day? It doesn't rain in Greece in the fall . . .

LIZA
It does in Berkeley. Maybe I'll bring you back with me.

AUGUST
You'd bring me back just to get rained on?

LIZA
Among other things . . .

AUGUST
Ho ho . . .

> AUGUST *drinks.*

LIZA *(quietly)*
Kiss me. Kiss me. Kiss me. Kiss me. Kiss me.

AUGUST
You *do* know Karl Marx was an inveterate wine drinker . . .

> AUGUST, *having not heard her, quickly kisses her head.*

LIZA
I didn't . . .

AUGUST
His family owned a vineyard. He used to make Engels ship bottles
of Bordeaux to him in, in London . . .

> A *small beat.* LIZA *drinks.*

AUGUST *(quietly)*
Touch me. Touch me. Touch me. Touch me.

      LIZA *places a hand* on AUGUST*'s thigh.*

LIZA
I have a. Small confession.

AUGUST
Should I be sober for this?

LIZA
It's small . . . I've never been to Budapest. PESHT.

AUGUST
What about Prague?

LIZA
Nope.

AUGUST
Romania, Italy . . .

LIZA
Nope, nope. Came straight here.

AUGUST
Well done, Polita. You had me fooled.

LIZA
I practiced on the boat over.

AUGUST
You are a wily woman.

LIZA
Thank you.

AUGUST
Not sure it was a compliment.

LIZA
I know.

> *A beat.*

AUGUST
Your hand is on my thigh, Liza.

LIZA
I know.

AUGUST
Do you plan on keeping it there?

LIZA
Hard to say.

AUGUST
Because I can't think straight with it there.

LIZA
Well I can't seem to move it.

AUGUST
I see.

> LIZA *moves her hand higher on* AUGUST's *thigh.*

LIZA
Move it yourself.

> AUGUST *slowly lifts her hand from his thigh and places it to his lips, closing his eyes.*
>
> AUGUST *kisses* LIZA's *fingers as though he is drinking her flesh.*
>
> *Then,* AUGUST *bites into* LIZA's *wrist, hard. She gasps a little in pain.*

LIZA (cont.) *(whisper)*
. . . harder . . .

A beat. AUGUST *removes his mouth from* LIZA'*s arm. A beat. He lifts his glass to his lips and takes a slow sip.*

LIZA *rubs her wrist.*

A long beat. AUGUST *does not look at* LIZA.

LIZA *(cont.)*
I can wait . . .

LIZA *stands and exits.*

AUGUST *remains onstage, drinking the remains of the bottle alone.*

Lights down.

ACT TWO

In the near fading darkness, we hear quietly, intimately, seductively, in voice-over:

AUGUST *(V.O.)*
Legend two. Zeus killed Semele accidentally with a lightning bolt, whoops, while she was carrying his child . . . the baby Dionysus. Zeus rescued the fetus from her belly and sliced open his own thigh, where he placed the child until it was ready to be born. Then he delivered the infant to the nymphs for them to raise. So Baby Dionysus . . . well, he had a touch of the kookies. Maybe because of the thigh. He had followers, a ragtag pack of satyrs, sileni, maenads, and nymphs, who danced and drank all the time, and were fierce and rowdy, and had bloody sacrificial rites to try to merge their identities with nature.

Maybe they weren't eating enough dirt.

> *Meanwhile, the lights slowly rise on* LIZA *in her pajamas. She makes her way to the table . . . or perhaps she is already there . . . After a long beat . . .*

LIZA
Legend three. (*A beat.*) Legend three. (*A beat.*) The third legend . . . Is . . .

> *Lights on full. It is morning on the vineyard.* LIZA *is once again alone. She is alone for quite a while. Troubled.*
>
> *Finally,* DAPHNE *enters with a bright expression on her face.*

DAPHNE

Kali Mera, Americaneetha. Would you like some Greek coffee? We also have Folders. The crystals.

LIZA

Fol-GERS.

DAPHNE

Fol-GERS, excuse me. You look very bad. As though you were awake all the night. So I will give you the Greek coffee. Thick and sweet and strong. Boy? *Agory?*

> BOY *enters.*

DAPHNE *(cont.)*

Yia-sou, agapi mou . . . Ehh, ftyakse tin Americaneetha ligo cafédaki, glyko, parakalo? Ke doseh-tin, ehh, yaourti me meli, ke . . . ligo psomi, ke . . . fruito. Meela, ne? (Hello love. Ehh, bring the American a little sweet coffee please? And bring her, ehh, yogurt with honey, and . . . a little bread, and . . . fruit. Apples, yes?)

BOY

Endaksi. (Okay.)

DAPHNE

Efharisto. (Thank you.)

> BOY *exits. A beat.*

DAPHNE *(cont.)*

Do you have any plans for the day?

LIZA

I don't know.

DAPHNE

The radio says there is a sale at an Italian shoe store at the Euro-center today. It is not far from here, but I do not drive so we would need *Avgusto* to driving us. I do not have much affection for the

Eurocenter, it is a bit coarse and smells like a swimming pool. But the stores are very good.

LIZA

I don't need shoes.

DAPHNE

Yes, but you may like to looking at them. Often I go and do not purchase anything, I just admire. It shall be dull here for you if we go . . .

      LIZA *looks around uncomfortably.*

DAPHNE *(cont.)*

You are uncomfortable with me still! Is this because you want to make love with my husband? To be frank, I was hoping you would last night. I am puzzled to why this did not occur. But do it soon, so perhaps we may all be more relaxed for your visit.

LIZA

Sorry?

DAPHNE

I am a very flexible woman. Which is where you and I differ, I believe. Also, I do not like violence during lovemaking, and I am sure he misses this sometimes . . .

LIZA

Uh . . . that's, / that's really.

DAPHNE

And I want to say this also: I will not continue to feed someone who insists on being my rival. I hope you understand.

LIZA

I do.

DAPHNE

Good.

AUGUST *enters, looking slightly hung over.*

DAPHNE *(cont.)*
Kali mera. (Good morning.) Your friend and I were just discussing you.

AUGUST
What were you discussing?

DAPHNE
I was saying I wished you had made love to her last night.

AUGUST
That's very adorable of you.

DAPHNE
I was saying you yearn to have sexual violence.

AUGUST
We can do without this over breakfast, *ne kota?* (yes chicken?)

DAPHNE
You are like a little sour boy. Does your head hurt from the *krassaki*? (wine)

AUGUST
Yes.

DAPHNE
I hope you shared some with your friend.

AUGUST
I did.

> BOY *enters with a tray filled with yogurt, apples, coffee, and bread.*

DAPHNE
There. We have yogurt, honey, apples, coffee, and fresh bread. The coffee is already sweetened. (*To* BOY.) *Ella, katse mazimas . . .* (Come here, sit down . . .)

BOY

Ohi . . . then pinao . . . (No . . . I'm not hungry . . .)

> BOY *moves off to the side and sets up a table with a manual juice press.*

AUGUST

Not hungry? That's a first . . .

DAPHNE

Is he sick? *Agory, ise arostos?* (Boy, are you sick?)

> BOY *shakes her head, retrieves a basket of fresh oranges to be juiced. She has her eye on* DAPHNE. DAPHNE *ignores her.*
>
> *All begin eating quietly, awkwardly.*
>
> *After a beat.*

DAPHNE *(cont.)*

If you are not too sleepy *Avgusto* I would like a ride to the Euro-center today. There is a sale on shoes.

AUGUST

We have no money, *kota.*

DAPHNE

I am just going to look. And your friend would like to come as well.

> AUGUST *looks at* LIZA.

AUGUST

You're going shopping together?

DAPHNE

And you do not have to shop with us. They are showing a movie in the cinema down the road. *The Raging Bull.* It is around a box-ing man.

> AUGUST *chuckles.*

DAPHNE *(cont.)*
Something is humorous?

AUGUST
Ah, no, well yes, the image of Liza buying shoes, actually.

DAPHNE
She wears shoes, does she not? *(To* LIZA.*)* You wear shoes, do you not?

LIZA
I wear shoes.

AUGUST
She doesn't want to do that, Liza, do you want to do that? Go shopping? At the Eurocenter?

LIZA
I do.

DAPHNE
And you have not seen a film in a while, so go to that and we will shop. And we will get a gift for Boy also, for working so hard this year.

> DAPHNE *smiles at* BOY. BOY *walks over to the radio and changes the station. Blondie's "Call Me" begins to play.*

DAPHNE *(cont.)*
He despises the folk music. It depresses him.

> BOY *turns the volume up and returns to her oranges, singing softly. She squeezes them with a manual press and dances somewhat sexily while doing so, feigning nonchalance . . . but clearly this is a performance for* DAPHNE.

> BOY *has no idea what she's singing.*

BOY
Kala meeya kala, baby

Kala meeya par
Kala meeya kala, danen
Ahno hooyoo-aahh
Kama pafya kala jah
Ano wayoh kame fra

Kal me (kal me) ala-lah
Kal me Kal me eneh eneh tah
Kal me (kal me) ala rah
You kan kal me eneh dayoh nai
Kal me

DAPHNE
He is so. What is the word? For when you need attention.

LIZA
I think I'll go shower . . . excuse me.

> LIZA *exits.*

> BOY *continues to dance, much more sexily. She takes her hat off.*

> DAPHNE*'s hand slides over to* AUGUST*'s. She tugs on it to make him watch too. He does. They eat.*

> *Juice drips down* BOY*'s arm. She licks it off.*

BOY
Kava mee weth ki-ses, bebee
Kava mee weth lah-ah
Rohl mee'een tizahna seetsa
Neveh kete nah
H'mo shaka nadoh nowah
Kava-ah lah vzahla baaaaaahhhhh

> DAPHNE *looks at* AUGUST.

DAPHNE
Shall we play a little?

AUGUST *(gesturing toward LIZA)*
She's right there . . .

    DAPHNE *pouts.* AUGUST *gives in.*

AUGUST **(cont.)** *(to DAPHNE)*
Stand up.

    She does.

AUGUST **(cont.)**
Walk over to her.

    She does.

AUGUST **(cont.)**
Touch her shoulder.

    She does.

AUGUST **(cont.)**
Kiss her neck.

    She does.

AUGUST **(cont.)**
Ask her what she wants.

DAPHNE *(to BOY)*
Ti thelis? (What do you want?)

BOY *(touching DAPHNE)*
Esena. (You.)

AUGUST *(to DAPHNE)*
Kiss her mouth.

    DAPHNE *kisses* BOY. BOY *begins to take off her clothes.*

AUGUST **(cont.)** *(gently, firmly)*
Ohi. Stamata. (No. Stop.)

    A beat. BOY *stops stripping.*

AUGUST *(cont.)*
Fee-yeh. (Go.)

BOY
Then katalaveno . . . (I don't understand . . .)

> *A beat.*

> BOY *skulks off.*

> DAPHNE *turns the radio off and pours herself a glass of juice.*

DAPHNE
Far too early in the day for *that*.

AUGUST
Indeed.

> *A beat.*

DAPHNE
You say that word so much. "Indeed."

AUGUST
I never / noticed.

DAPHNE
It is a way of shutting down.

AUGUST
A what?

DAPHNE
You affirm something indirectly, and therefore it ends the discussion. "Indeed." My father used that word all the time in English. It makes my fingers clench the air.

AUGUST
I won't say it again.

> DAPHNE *sits.*

AUGUST *(cont.)*
I've never seen you like this, *kota*. It's kind of thrilling.

> *A beat.*

DAPHNE
I want to ask you something *Avgusto* and I am not interested in the truth but it is important for me to say these words out loud so I have the memory of them hanging.

AUGUST
If you aren't interested in the truth, chicken, what do you expect me to say?

DAPHNE
Your closest approximation.

AUGUST
I'll do my best . . .

DAPHNE
I want to know if you will make love with that woman.

AUGUST
Will I make love to Liza. I wish I knew how to answer that.

DAPHNE
Try slowly, with feeling.

> *A beat.*

AUGUST
I want to say this: "No, Daphne. No I will not." I *want* to say it. (*A beat.*) She isn't beautiful you know, traditionally. Her face is . . . Kind of saggy? She doesn't take care of herself. Not like you. And she's, she sort of reeks of damage, which is.

DAPHNE
Yes?

AUGUST

I don't know. You know when Liza, when she—You don't want to hear this.

DAPHNE

I very much do.

AUGUST

When she, she um climaxes . . . she cries. Every single time. I'm not talking little vanity tears, I'm talking these gasping terrifying sobs. First time it happened I thought I had hurt her. Because she kept asking me to go harder, harder. And then she's bawling, she can't breathe, and me, "I'm sorry I'm so sorry" and. And she says, "It's not the pain. It's the mortality."

DAPHNE

I see. So making love to Liza is like making love to death. You are attracted to death.

AUGUST

No no, the opposite . . . there's this tiny little pea-sized hunger spinning beneath it all . . . when you get *that* close to it, I mean— it's impossible to talk about.

DAPHNE

I see. And how does it feel to making love with me?

AUGUST

Making love with you. You.

DAPHNE

I.

AUGUST

You're very quiet, first of all. And delicate. I could shatter you.

DAPHNE

Oh.

AUGUST

And you take your time, none of the rushing urgency that. Um your fingers aren't clamps, they're feathers, and. (*A beat.*) You make me feel massive. Like a conquistador!

DAPHNE

You enjoy her more.

AUGUST

No no it's just / different.

DAPHNE

Do you imagine her when we make love?

AUGUST

No. Sometimes.

DAPHNE

Oh.

AUGUST

I picture her hair greasy. You don't sweat, Daphne. Did you know this?

DAPHNE

I.

AUGUST

Ever. I've never seen you sweat.

DAPHNE

Oh.

AUGUST

I picture her sweating. I picture her nails cutting into my arms.

DAPHNE

Oh.

AUGUST

Not all the time, okay. Just when I feel a little. Ah lost.

DAPHNE
Oh.

AUGUST
So.

DAPHNE
Oh.

AUGUST
Are you. Okay?

DAPHNE
No.

AUGUST
Will you be?

DAPHNE
No.

> DAPHNE *picks up a knife from the table and stabs herself in the womb. She doubles over in pain, but a moment later, she rights herself as though nothing has happened.*
>
> *A beat. They eat in silence.*

DAPHNE *(cont.)*
I want to ask you something *Avgusto* and I am not interested in the truth but it is important for me to say these words out loud so I have the memory of them hanging.

AUGUST
If you aren't interested in the truth, chicken, what do you expect me to say?

DAPHNE
Your closest approximation.

AUGUST
I'll do my best . . .

DAPHNE
I want to know if you will make love with that woman.

AUGUST
Will I make love to Liza. No, Daphne. No I will not.

DAPHNE
Good. Because she breaks me.

> *They continue to eat in silence. Lights down.*
>
> *Time passes. It is late afternoon. The stage is soaked in November's melting Mediterranean light, buttery and lush and wicked.*
>
> DAPHNE *enters, ecstatic. She carries a large fancy shopping bag.*
>
> LIZA *and* AUGUST *follow happily.*

DAPHNE *(cont.)*
Ah! That was precisely what I needed! My spirit is refreshed! Do you not feel this way, Liza?

LIZA
I do, Daphne. Like a weight has been lifted.

DAPHNE
Yes! And always after shopping I have a small hilarity in my throat when I return home and remove clothing from bags. I have obsession for texture, I think. Touching different leathers. This one is tough, this one is soft and wrinkled, this one is like glass . . . and simply nothing compares to the smell of something new . . .

LIZA
It's a great feeling . . .

> AUGUST *cheerily pours himself a whiskey.*

AUGUST
Whiskey, / anyone?

LIZA
Sure!

DAPHNE
It is affirming. I can phrase it no other way. Placing a new good thing on your body. In a manner it is saying, you are a good body. Liza, I must tell you again, I do not often accept gifts from people I do not know well. This holds a very warm place in me.

LIZA
Oh, / now.

DAPHNE
I want to keep saying. Your generosity is was unexpected but and also unnecessary, and I feel very touched by it.

LIZA
Well you're cooking for me and everything, so.

DAPHNE
It does not to equal this. You are a gracious / woman.

AUGUST *(laughing)*
Okay, enough! Are we getting a fashion show or what?

> DAPHNE *scampers away giddily.* AUGUST *hands* LIZA *a drink.*

AUGUST *(cont.)*
Well *that* was the quickest way to my wife's heart.

LIZA
You're welcome.

> *They clink glasses and drink.*

AUGUST
I feel like I need an acid bath to burn that place off me. God the WASTE! And that FOUNTAIN! They need an enormous spouting pool of water when they have the ocean two miles down?

LIZA
Some European developer's wet dream. So to speak.

AUGUST
And that huge tacky Parthenon-y façade . . . that alone probably cost a fortune. Goddamn it. If I had that kind of money I'd—

LIZA
You'd what.

AUGUST
I'd . . . seriously? How much are we talking?

LIZA
Millions. Many.

> AUGUST *thinks.*

AUGUST
Wow. Huh. Okay gimmie a second . . . This is now, right?

LIZA
Tomorrow, say.

AUGUST
Here?

LIZA
In the States. California.

AUGUST
Um. Okay. Who do we have on our side?

LIZA
The ACLU?

AUGUST
Perfect! So this is a me and you thing!

LIZA
Yeah. I'm the Ike to your Tina!

AUGUST

Love it. Great. What about Danny B.? You still talk to him?

LIZA

He moved to LA and planted a family.

AUGUST

Fuck. Well, we're loaded, right? We'll relocate them to the Bay Area and get cranking on his old lobbyist contacts. Get a paid full-time staff. A REAL office. One with air conditioning this time. Mobilize a *full-scale* grassroots lobbyist movement.

LIZA *(triumphant)*

That's him. That's my August.

AUGUST *(deeply serious)*

We'll bring that motherfucking slimy-haired geriatric turkey-necked Bible-thumping actor-cowboy down to his knobby arthritic knees.

LIZA

We sure as fucking hell will . . .

> LIZA *rushes to grab her purse, energized. She pulls out a beat-up, much-read paperback. The face of Ronald Reagan adorns the cover.*

AUGUST

You saved this.

LIZA

Remember what you wrote inside?

AUGUST

"To My Lascivious Something. Suck on this. Love, Mega-Marx."

LIZA

No, in the margins.

> AUGUST *flips through the book.*

AUGUST
My manifesto.

LIZA
Yup. And a game plan. For when we got to Berkeley. And some notes from our rallies, talking points and stuff . . .

AUGUST *(reading, mountainous)*
"There comes a time when the apparatus is so corrupt, so sickening, that you have no choice but to act. And you've got to seize the levers, take hold and scream at the edge of your voices to those who run it, scream that unless they hear you, the engine will be stalled." Ha! Now *this* is something my kid could be proud of.

LIZA
You're right, he would.

> LIZA *approaches* AUGUST *warmly.*

> AUGUST *closes the book and hands it back to her.*

AUGUST
He'll be proud of the vineyard too.

> *A beat.*

LIZA
The what?

AUGUST
You know most people equate *wine* with *wealth.* They see wine drinkers as like a *type,* going to tastings, getting—buying magazines . . . *because.* They fall prey to an, to a hackneyed and patently Western notion of class identity. THAT is a travesty, in my opinion. Wine has the potential to be a true, a true populist . . .

> *Searching.* LIZA *gives him nothing.*

AUGUST *(cont.)*
And this country has so much potential. We're no longer under foreign governance, we're joining the EC next year, we elected a

democratic president in May . . . who knows, in twenty to thirty years, Greece could become . . . (*Still searching.*) And I'll tell you something Liza, it feels so goddamn good to be in on the ground level. I can actually *do* something. Build something with my bare hands. You can't build jack shit back home without piles of money. It's a dead country. No offense.

LIZA

You left the States so you could save Greece? Because I thought you blew your life savings on a beverage and had nowhere else to go.

AUGUST

That's not why we / left the States.

LIZA

Because you found a woman who kinda STEAMS with privilege, who just *happened* to come with a huge chunk of free land . . .

AUGUST

Well that's true—

LIZA

And now you're indulging a wine fetish and calling it activism. So, like, if I handed you a wad of cash right now, you'd what. Mobilize a grassroots lobbyist movement in California? Or bury it in the dirt with those fucking grapes?

AUGUST

I—

LIZA

Who are you, August?

> *A beat.*

> DAPHNE *promenades into their view. She is wearing a gorgeous sparkly gown and high heels.*

> *A beat as they take her in. She is beyond stunning.*

AUGUST *(amazed, quietly)*
Daphne.

DAPHNE
Voila! I am a holiday!

> LIZA *applauds and hoots.*

LIZA
Hoo, dang! Bravo! Bravo! August you are one lucky son of a bitch . . .

AUGUST
Ehis klepsi to pnevma-mou . . . (You have stolen my breath . . .)

DAPHNE
That is the most beautiful thing you have said to me . . .

LIZA
What did he say?

DAPHNE
He says I have stolen his breath . . . but the word *pnevma*, it also means spirit . . . I have stolen his spirit . . .

LIZA
Quite a dress!

DAPHNE
A designer from Paris. He is very famous. So famous no one can afford his clothing!

AUGUST
Liza. How much money did you spend on my wife today?

LIZA
What difference does it make?

AUGUST
I'd like to know.

LIZA

That doesn't answer my question at / all, August. What *difference* does it really make how much I spent on your wife, it's spent. Gone.

AUGUST *(overlapping, slowly)*

I'm not interested in answering your question, I'm interested in knowing how much money you spent on my wife.

LIZA

Twelve hundred dollars.

> *A beat.* DAPHNE *tries to maintain her poise, but she is ashamed.*

AUGUST

Um.

LIZA

She fell in love with the dress. It looked delightful on her. She said she hadn't had a new dress in. Seven years, I think? I thought to myself, now THAT is an outrage. So I did what I could to help.

AUGUST

Could, ah. Someone please explain to me how this transaction occurred.

LIZA

What do / you mean?

AUGUST

Step by step. Who said what, who asked / for what.

DAPHNE

You spent twice the cost on her last night. (*A small beat.*) I will take it / off.

AUGUST *(smoldering)*

No no, don't bother. I'm sure it'll come in quite handy. We have a SLEW of functions coming up. Society balls, galas, et cetera. God forbid we show up looking like village trash. Speaking of, maybe you should show off your new wardrobe to your people down the way?

DAPHNE *is quiet.*

AUGUST *(cont.)*
No people? Ah well. They'll come around. (*To* LIZA.) Daphne doesn't get along with her people. She had an incident. Did you tell your new friend about the incident?

DAPHNE
Avgusto.

AUGUST
Daphne had an incident with / someone in the village.

DAPHNE
Meen ise toso malakas. (Don't be such a bastard.)

AUGUST *(confidentially, to LIZA)*
Daphne's particularly. It's very sweet, actually. Sensitive to beautiful things. And beautiful people. Better look out, next thing you know she'll have her tongue between your legs too. (*A beat. Immediate and genuine regret.*) Jesus. That was horrible. Fuck. I don't know what I'm thinking. Excuse me.

AUGUST *exits.*

DAPHNE
He is unbearably touchy about money. Do not let it affect you.

LIZA
I didn't.

DAPHNE
Oh. (*A small beat.*) Well. It is good we celebrate today. Tomorrow shall be a day of mourning.

LIZA
Mourning? Why?

DAPHNE
The tasting. Oh Liza. His wine will not be good. It will be very sweet, very quick on the tongue. Very simple.

LIZA
What?

DAPHNE
The heat that harvest four years ago was exceptional and he picked his grapes too late. When the grapes are too ripe you get jam, not wine. He has no idea.

LIZA
Well he seems to know what he's doing, so . . .

DAPHNE
Now he does. His technique is improved.

LIZA
Still. There's no telling how it'll turn out.

DAPHNE
I have tasted it. Last week. Against his knowledge.

LIZA
. . . last night . . .

DAPHNE
I did not drink last night to show a point. Women must do the small dishonest things sometimes in order to retain our presence . . . You understand this.

LIZA
No uh, I only do big dishonest things . . .

> DAPHNE *smiles.*

DAPHNE
I like you a good deal more than I did yesterday. And my dress looks fabulous on me. And tonight we shall have glamour and elation. And we shall make *Avgusto* with wearing the suit he was married to me. You will find him beautiful, Liza.

LIZA
I already do.

DAPHNE
MORE beautiful.

LIZA
Not possible.

DAPHNE
We are lucky women to be company with such a man . . .

LIZA
Indeed.

>   *A small beat.*

DAPHNE
Indeed.

>   BOY *appears, smiling lopsidedly. She is very very drunk.*
>   DAPHNE *grabs a shopping bag and approaches her.*

DAPHNE *(cont.)*
Agapi mou! Ela'tho. Sou efera thoro. (My love! Come here. I have
something for you.)

>   BOY *approaches* DAPHNE, *smiling.* DAPHNE *opens a bag*
>   *and pulls out a record.*

DAPHNE *(cont.)*
Rotisa ton andra sto magazi yia "Blondie." Mou to edose afto . . . "Eat
to the Beat." Simeni "Fa'eh sto rythmo." (I asked the man in the shop
for "Blondie." He gave that to me . . . "Eat to the Beat." It means
"Eat to the Beat.")

>   DAPHNE *mimes eating to the beat.*

>   BOY *takes the record and strokes the cover. She glows with*
>   *love, but then stumbles drunkenly and smashes into the table.*

DAPHNE *(cont.)* *(laughing)*
He is so drunk!

LIZA
Kids! What can ya do.

> BOY *gathers herself, then leans over to kiss* DAPHNE *on the mouth.* DAPHNE *turns her cheek to* BOY. BOY *receives a mouthful of hair.*

> DAPHNE *glances at* LIZA *uncomfortably.*

> BOY *is extremely hurt by this gesture. She hurls the record across the room.*

DAPHNE
Agapi! (Love!)

BOY *(screaming)*
Yiati then me kitas san teen kitas? Yiati? (Why don't you look at me like you look at her?)

DAPHNE
Agapi . . . (Love . . .)

> BOY *begins to cry.* DAPHNE *goes to her and* BOY *tears herself away and lunges at* LIZA, *spitting at her.* LIZA *gasps.*

BOY
Se miso! Fee'yeh, Fee'yeh! (I hate you! Leave! Leave!)

DAPHNE
Ohi! Ohi! Ftani! Ohi! (No! No! Enough! No!)

> DAPHNE *tears* BOY *off* LIZA. BOY *stumbles to the side and throws up.*

DAPHNE *(cont.)*
Oh . . . agapi mou . . . (Oh . . . my love. . .)

> DAPHNE *grabs a tissue and cleans* BOY's *face.*

BOY

Me pezees ke me pezees . . . (You play me and play me . . .)

DAPHNE

Shhh . . .

> DAPHNE *strokes* BOY's *hair and rocks her.* LIZA *checks herself to make sure she isn't hurt.*

DAPHNE *(cont.)*

Please forgive him / Liza, he.

LIZA *(vicious)*

What the fuck . . .

> *A beat.*

DAPHNE

Pardon?

LIZA

Are you messing around with her like she's some kind of a . . . a /

DAPHNE

This is not your concern, I am afraid.

LIZA

If you're abusing that child it's no longer a private matter.

DAPHNE

Some might call it giving pleasure.

LIZA

Does she look pleased?

DAPHNE

She is ill from too much drink.

LIZA

She is in LOVE with you.

DAPHNE

You truly find this tragic? Or are you having the classic American preoccupation with morality?

LIZA

CHRIST, the self-indulgent, uh so-called love for beauty, you / are POISONING her!

DAPHNE

This is perfect Liza, the way your mouth opens and words tumble out and you have no filter for your brain.

LIZA

And him! He used to be so, so HUGE, but now he's like a stump, and you're standing there like it's something to be proud of.

> *A beat.* DAPHNE *continues stroking* BOY's *hair.*

DAPHNE *(coolly)*

Liza. Have I told you that I adore my dress?

LIZA

You have.

DAPHNE

I adore it so much that I shall continue to wear it regardless of the vulgar person who paid for it. And thank you for the sermon. Now I have tending to other matters. Excuse me.

> DAPHNE *stumbles off with* BOY.

> LIZA *stands. She walks around the space, a bit manic. She retrieves her bag from the corner of the porch.*

> *She reaches into her bag and pulls out a much-viewed photograph.*

> AUGUST *emerges, looking beaten.*

AUGUST

Where's Daphne?

LIZA

The um. The teenager had a bit of a meltdown.

> LIZA *points to the corner where* BOY *threw up.* AUGUST
> *investigates.* LIZA *tucks the photograph into her pocket.*

AUGUST

Oh man. Sorry about that. He's at an awkward age. Hormones raging . . . no real family . . . (*A small beat.*) I hope you aren't hungry. Dinner could be a while—

LIZA

Your wine will be terrible.

> *A small beat.*

AUGUST

Sorry, I didn't hear you.

LIZA

YOUR WINE WILL BE TERRIBLE.

AUGUST

I didn't hear you.

LIZA

It will—it will be terrible.

AUGUST

I'm not comprehending you.

LIZA

Your, your wine, it / won't be.

AUGUST

No comprende.

LIZA

It will be / ter, ter.

AUGUST

I can't hear you.

LIZA
Ter, just bad, your wine.

AUGUST
Sorry, what did you say?

A small beat.

LIZA
Nothing.

AUGUST
You said / some.

LIZA
I was talking to myself.

Another long beat. AUGUST *glances back toward the house.*

AUGUST
I hope you aren't hungry. Dinner could be a while—

LIZA
I'm not hungry.

AUGUST
We'll eat like real Greeks, at midnight . . .

He rubs his head in exhaustion. She approaches him, her hand outstretched. He backs away.

AUGUST *(cont.)*
Look, we're taking all that crap back to the store tomorrow, the / shoes, everything.

LIZA
I don't want her to take anything back. / They were gifts.

AUGUST
Liza. Why the. WHY would you ever EVER spend twelve hundred dollars on clothing for my wife?

LIZA
Because I can. (*A beat.*) I'm, I have. A lot.

> *A beat.*

AUGUST
Of money.

LIZA
Yes.

AUGUST
When you say "a lot," I mean, / what are?

LIZA
Sixty million dollars.

> *Another beat.* AUGUST *is floored.*

AUGUST
Did you hit the fucking lottery, or . . .

LIZA
Not really.

AUGUST
Then . . .

LIZA
It's a bit of an anecdote, uh . . . a *legend*, actually . . .

AUGUST
An inheritance, what . . . ?

LIZA
Kind of . . .

> *A long expectant beat.*

AUGUST
Are you gonna tell me?

LIZA

Um. I think I should be holding you when I do.

> LIZA *approaches* AUGUST *and touches him gently.*

AUGUST

Jesus. Listen, Liza. I have to ask you to leave. First thing in the morning. I'm sorry. It's just better. For everyone.

LIZA

I can't—

AUGUST

I am going to be a father in exactly twenty-five weeks and four days. I'm not going to blow this. I don't want to and I'm not going to. Do you understand?

LIZA

No.

AUGUST

Good.

> *A beat.*

> LIZA *pulls the photograph out of her pocket and looks down at it.*

> *She hands it to* AUGUST.

AUGUST

What's this?

LIZA

Graduation from middle school. He just turned fourteen. It was raining.

> *Suddenly, anything breakable in the vicinity shatters at once—frames, vases, glasses, potted plants.*

> *Neither* LIZA *nor* AUGUST *notices.*

> *A long stare.*

AUGUST *(small voice)*
What . . .

LIZA
I know. It's scary sometimes. And his laugh is exactly the same as yours too, that sardonic snort when he's feeling superior. And he's a terrible dancer. He talks in his sleep like you do. Um, what else . . .

AUGUST *(quietly)*
What are you showing me . . .

LIZA
And he. Doesn't cry. *(A beat.)* He is a punched hole. He is a fallen leaf. He is made of light. He really is. Blue sparks in my mouth and yours when we made him, we were chewing and screwing in the dark because the sparks turned us on.

AUGUST
We made a boy.

LIZA
Out of light. *(A beat.)* I will tell you the legend now.

AUGUST
Look at / him, my God.

LIZA
My legend, August. It's my only legend . . .

> *The air somehow changes . . . the lights melt . . .*

> BOY *appears, as a boy. He is dressed in a graduation robe. He moves delicately, deliberately, much different than the slouchy street urchin of earlier.*

> *He speaks softly, in a deep voice.*

BOY
July 28, 1978. Your mouth is chomping Wint-o-Green after Wint-o-Green right now. You're in the kitchen surrounded by

bills. I can hear you through the vents as I write this. You chew faster when you're anxious. Maybe you're chewing as you read this. Illegible. Crossed-out.

I know this is sloppy but I wanted to preserve each thought as it left my pen to give an accurate record of illegible. Crossed-out crossed-out scribble wanted to.

But first, business. You should sell anything that has some value, like my bike and my records and my books. Not my hi-fi. The left speaker is broken. I left my pot in the top drawer for you, but it's kind of old. Scribble scribble crossed-out forget it, that wasn't funny. My clothes are probably worthless, they were when we bought them.

Now here's the crossed-out part. I know we said I'd try but illegible crossed-out illegible not changing, nothing changes and it won't. Like remember how I had that so-called breakthrough and I told Dr. Randy that the world felt fake, and that I was the only one who knew it was fake? I still feel this way, but it's much worse now because crossed-out scribble sorry, my knuckle hurts.

BOY *moves his knuckle the way* AUGUST *did earlier.*

BOY *(cont.)*
But knowing this is not true and feeling it in my heart are two different things.

   And I can't stop, I play every single scenario over and over in my head only it's worse now because I do it over really small things. "If I brush my teeth this morning, THIS will happen. If I don't, THIS will happen." Or like, "If I blink my left eye, THIS will happen. If I blink my right, THIS will." And then I think, if all the different outcomes for every single tiny thing are endless, how can ANYTHING be real? And then the ringing starts just like before and then I get weightless and I'm shaking and throwing up again. And the crossed-out panic doesn't ever illegible. Especially at night. My heart beats so hard my eyeballs bounce. It would be cool if it didn't make me illegible.

You just yawned really loud. It was funny. In a few seconds your head will be on the table, and you'll be drooling onto the phone bill. I'll touch your head on my way out, so maybe you'll still feel my hand there when you wake up.

Oh, do you remember Colleen, the girl from the Y who used to write with her toes to impress people? You were right, I did have sex with her. But only once. She smelled like paper. I always felt bad about that lie.

Don't save this letter, okay mom? Just read it once. Then burn it.

Love you,
August

> BOY *freezes somewhere on stage.*

LIZA

I've heard that drowning is painless. You just have to fight the urge to breathe. But I guess he did that a long time ago, so. Um. A state-owned campground near Tahoe, there's this lake with this. Boat ramp. On either side of the ramp is a ledge with a sudden drop-off. When the water is high you can't see it. Two kids drowned in that exact spot the previous summer . . . Um he wanted to make it seem like an accident for my sake, so . . . So a, a citizen's coalition had been trying to convince the state for years to erect a fence or a concrete barrier around the ramp, but they were roundly ignored . . . so this of course sent them in a tizzy. And the papers went nuts.

I, uh, filed a wrongful death suit. Got every penny I asked for. The publicity helped of course . . . I didn't talk to anyone, reporters, neighbors . . . When the cameras were around, which was like EVERY DAY for a while, I just. Hid my face with my hair.

Oh and I. Burned the note.

> BOY *disappears. A beat.*

LIZA *(cont.)*

The ultimate screwing of the system, right? (*A long beat.*) What, ah. What are you thinking?

AUGUST

I'm backing up in my brain to yesterday morning, before you got here, I'm trying to. See how I felt then because. Because I don't think I'll ever get that feeling back.

LIZA

He is the roots and we are the leaves. Now we have to rebuild from what he left us. We're gonna use that sixty million and we're gonna bring that motherfucking actor cowboy down to his arthritic knees.

AUGUST *(quietly)*

I wasn't there for him . . .

LIZA

Come home, August. This is not you. You are a MOUNTAIN. Everything here . . . It's ersatz. It doesn't exist.

> *She strokes him. He leans into her.*

AUGUST

. . . I *AM* home . . .

LIZA

No, August. I am your home.

AUGUST

I wish you had never come . . . I wish you weren't here now . . . I want you to leave and never ever think of me again, never come near me, or my wife, or my baby . . .

I hate you Liza . . . do you understand / these words . . .

LIZA

You hate yourself . . .

> *He turns away. She stands, and slowly removes her shirt. She's in her bra.*

AUGUST
This isn't a game . . .

LIZA
I know . . .

AUGUST
Fucking pack your shit and leave . . .

> *She bites him hard on the neck. He pushes her back, begins tearing at her clothes viscously and kissing her everywhere. He is wild . . .*

AUGUST *(cont.)*
You you you you you . . .

> *After a bit, he begins to break down, bawling. They remain like that, sprawled across each other, clothes ripped, him crying on top of her. He rolls off.*

> *After a moment,* LIZA *stands and removes her shoes. She removes her jeans. She removes her bra and panties. She leaves them in a pile on the floor. A beat.*

LIZA
I'm going for a walk, August. I am going to walk down to your vines. I am going to lie down in the dirt. And I will wait there for you. I will wait there until you come to me. And if you never come, I will still wait.

> *She exits.*

> AUGUST *sits still a moment. He wipes the tears off his face and clears his throat. He pours himself a whiskey. He sits back down in the chair and stares ahead for a while, not drinking.*

> DAPHNE *enters, still wearing her sparkly gown.*

DAPHNE
Well. Boy is passed out finally. Your friend I am sure spoke of the incident . . .

AUGUST
Yeah . . .

DAPHNE
She is where?

AUGUST
She . . . went for a walk . . .

DAPHNE
Your rudeness to me gave her power. I do not want to be in the same room with her again. She is a troubled woman I understand, but she insults me continually and I cannot remain dignity. *Retain.* Please when she returns tell her to leave by tomorrow. I will cook dinner tonight but she must find breakfast herself. I will eat in the kitchen if you must have her as company out here . . . what is on your neck?

> DAPHNE *approaches* AUGUST.

DAPHNE *(cont.)*
You're bleeding . . . how did . . .

> DAPHNE *realizes these are teeth marks. She sees* LIZA's *clothes heaped on the floor.*

DAPHNE *(cont.)*
No, *agapi* . . .

AUGUST
I need a moment, please.

DAPHNE *(quietly furious)*
Of course you do. And you have been crying. This is all very emotional.

AUGUST
Please, Daphne, just give me a moment alone.

DAPHNE
Yes, you will get your moment alone, you will get many of them. This I would not have predicted. I thought more self-respect from

you. No, naturally this happened, it is exactly right. You have a coward in you. It is your ugliest part. Could you not have held yourself? Are you so stinking with desire that you cannot smell what an animal she is?

AUGUST
You can think what you want, and I, at this moment. I can't help you.

DAPHNE
What do you mean?

AUGUST
Go.

DAPHNE
What do you mean? What do you mean?

AUGUST
Please. Go downstairs.

DAPHNE
I want to understand / what you have just told me . . .

AUGUST *(quietly)*
Go. Go.

DAPHNE
I will not . . .

> AUGUST *smashes his whiskey on the table, loudly. A beat.*
>
> DAPHNE, *quietly, and with dignity, exits.*
>
> AUGUST *stares ahead a moment. His eyes soon shift to the pile of* LIZA's *clothes. He stands and approaches them. He picks them up and begins to walk toward the direction in which* LIZA *exited.*
>
> *He stops, stares ahead. He returns to his seat, still holding her clothes. He drinks his whiskey. He does nothing.*
>
> *Night falls, the stage darkens.* AUGUST *remains outside.*

Morning. AUGUST's head is resting on the pile of LIZA's clothes. The bottle of whiskey is nearly empty.

AUGUST awakens. He rubs his eyes and his head. He looks around groggily. Birds chirp, a far-off rooster crows. It is morning. He has slept outside all night.

LIZA enters, still naked. Her back is covered in dirt.

A beat.

He holds out her clothes to her. She takes them but does not dress immediately.

LIZA
I. Couldn't keep waiting. I got cold.

AUGUST
Would you like a towel?

LIZA
No.

> *A beat.*

AUGUST
She'll be up any second.

LIZA
August, I want to hear you tell / me what you've.

AUGUST
I just, I think it will be best if you have your clothes on when she comes up.

LIZA
Oh. Of course . . .

> LIZA *dresses.*

> DAPHNE *enters in her robe and sees* LIZA *putting on her clothes.*

DAPHNE

Well. You are both still here. *Avgusto*, my nerves are very slight. If you have made a decision, please invoke it and either spare me your faces or let us get on with our day.

> *A long beat.*

> AUGUST *turns to* DAPHNE.

AUGUST

I'm sorry.

DAPHNE *(quietly furious)*

That's it? (*A beat.*) Understand this. You will never know your child, *Avgusto*. You are a father who is dead.

> *She hands him her wedding ring and exits. A beat.*

LIZA

Are you okay?

AUGUST

No.

LIZA

Will you be?

AUGUST

No.

> DAPHNE *returns.*

DAPHNE

Well. You are both still here. *Avgusto*, my nerves are very slight. If you have made a decision, please invoke it and either spare me your faces or let us get on with our day.

> *A long beat.*

> AUGUST *turns to* LIZA.

AUGUST
I'm sorry.

LIZA
Okay, great. (*To* DAPHNE.) Lovely meeting you.

> LIZA *hands the Reagan book to* AUGUST.

LIZA *(cont.)*
Guess I won't be needing this. But *you* might. In case you need to remind yourself of who you could be. If you weren't such a fucking coward.

> LIZA *exits. A beat.*

DAPHNE
Are you okay?

AUGUST
No.

DAPHNE
Will you be?

AUGUST
No.

> DAPHNE *disappears.*
>
> *A long long beat. The air fills with sound.*

ANNOUNCER
In other news . . . things often burst.

> *The sound builds.*
>
> BOY/AUGUST JR. *enters in cap and gown again, swigging from a bottle. He carries dirt.*
>
> *Slowly,* AUGUST *approaches* BOY.
>
> *Blackout. End of play.*

ROADKILL
CONFIDENTIAL

PRODUCTION HISTORY

Roadkill Confidential had its world premiere on September 7, 2010, at 3LD Art & Technology Center in a production by Clubbed Thumb. Director: Kip Fagan. Set design: Peter Ksander. Costume design: Jessica Pabst. Lighting design: Jeanette Yew. Sound design: Bart Fasbender. Production manager: Brendan Regimbal. Stage manager: Sunny Stapleton. Sculpture artist: Jessica Scott. Props: Miranda King. Video design: Shaun Irons and Lauren Petty.

TREVOR	Rebecca Henderson
WILLIAM/TV ANNOUNCER/DOCTOR	Greg McFadden
RANDY/FRIZZY-HAIRED MAN	Alex Alfanger
MELANIE	Polly Lee
FBI MAN	Danny Mastriogiorgio

CHARACTERS

TREVOR	female, thirty, furtive and glamorous
WILLIAM/TV ANNOUNCER/DOCTOR	male, mid forties, balding, dorky, well-meaning
RANDY/FRIZZY-HAIRED MAN	male, teens/early twenties, wiry and manic
MELANIE	female, late thirties to early forties, bubbly and shrill
FBI MAN	male, thirties to forties, cool, level, dangerous, mysterious, jaded

SETTING

A small New England county, upstate New York.

A road.

A dark nondescript room.

TIME

The end of fall, moving into the winter.

NOTES

The setting should not be real, or naturalistic. It should not be a set for the piece to play within but rather something against which the piece can resonate: more installation than set.

Punctuation set within parenthesis (. . .) (???) (!!!) is used to indicate a gesture or some sort of vocal sound appropriate to the character and the situation. It is not a realistic sound, however.

The installation will begin as something simple, but will transform throughout the play, perhaps during the transitions at the hands of Trevor, until ultimately the entire playing space and beyond is one enormous diorama. Part of the space is dedicated to a screen or monitor on which we see the FBI Man's live feed.

PLEASE NOTE: Trevor is on stage for the entire duration. When not specifically noted, she is working, watching television, and reacting to it all. She is especially present on stage whenever the FBI Man is talking, whether lit specially, or in her own realm of movement and expression.

All scene titles are projected.

The FBI MAN *appears . . . sinister, weary, commanding.*

FBI MAN
You could say it all began five months ago

But that's not where I'll start
I'll start *before* it started

On a radiant Tuesday morning
In the lazy days of late spring

Trevor was contemplating her next project.
She didn't know what form it would take
Nor how much time
Nor even what material
She only knew
It was to be brutal.

>TREVOR *is in her studio, watching TV news, as she does throughout the play.*

FBI MAN *(cont.)*
Who is Trevor, you ask?
She might have been my greatest triumph.
But she was my demise.
So to speak.

>TREVOR *flips the channels. Lots of violence. She settles on one station.*

>*A* TV ANNOUNCER*'s voice is heard.*

TV ANNOUNCER
And in sadder news
A child has died in the Berkshires this week

Seven-year-old Callie Stewart touched a wild bunny
Outside her home in Austerlitz
The animal was infected with a rare bacterial disease
Causing Callie to perish within mere days.
The name of the disease is being withheld
For reasons of national security

But let it be known, Berkshire residents
The bunny has been detained.

You are in no danger.

>   TREVOR *is suddenly in her car, driving.*
>
>   THUMP. *Squeal of tires. She pulls over.*
>
>   *She has hit a bunny accidentally. She stares at it. Emotion: compassion, revulsion, fascination, etc.*
>
>   *She retrieves a camera and photographs the bunny dying. Then—she gets an idea. She puts on a pair of work gloves.*

FBI MAN
Jump cut.
>   Five months later
>   Trevor is in bed with a frizzy-haired man.

• *One Month Ago: Rubber Face*

>   TREVOR *is in her studio, now in bed with her lover, a* FRIZZY-HAIRED MAN. *They are frozen.*
>
>   *The* FRIZZY-HAIRED MAN *is playing with* TREVOR*'s face.*
>
>   *Everything around them is covered in tarps.*
>
>   TREVOR *is staring at a flickering TV with the sound off.*

FRIZZY-HAIRED MAN
Rubber-face

TREVOR
I'm trying to think of a way to tell you to stop that
    Without using the words "aggravating" or "retarded"

FRIZZY-HAIRED MAN
Ha!
    Sorry.
    I'll make coffee?
    Should I make coffee?
(*He finds a piece of paper.*)
    What is this?
(*He reads.*)
"Friendly Fire
    The Roadside Explosives
    Mortar Rounds
    The Drive-bys
    The Ethnic Cleanse
    Checkpoint Fuckyou"

TREVOR
Band names

FRIZZY-HAIRED MAN
Who's in a band?

TREVOR
No one
    I couldn't sleep.
    Nightmares
    My hands were like this the whole time

FRIZZY-HAIRED MAN (*flips the paper over and reads*)
"Thanks for the help. You're a swell kid. Sorry it didn't work out.
With Affection, Trevor."

TREVOR
That's from yesterday
    I thought you were leaving much sooner

FRIZZY-HAIRED MAN
What did you eat for lunch yesterday?

TREVOR
Why?

FRIZZY-HAIRED MAN
Because sometimes what you eat
    Like eating badly affects your dreams
    The shattering of one's self-image

TREVOR
You're much cuter when you're focused on pleasing me

FRIZZY-HAIRED MAN
I need a little break
    My jaw hurts

TREVOR
All right
    I'll tell you what I dreamed, then

FRIZZY-HAIRED MAN
Please

TREVOR
I was the keeper of the marvel

FRIZZY-HAIRED MAN
Wow.
    You aren't ordinary.

TREVOR
I know.

The FRIZZY-HAIRED MAN *kisses* TREVOR. *He is about to turn off the TV.*

TREVOR *(cont.)*
Don't touch that.

FRIZZY-HAIRED MAN
Okay
    I'm so happy to be here—

TREVOR
What about my coffee?

FRIZZY-HAIRED MAN
Right. Sorry. (*He stands.*) Ow.

TREVOR
Your back
    Poor thing
    I have Advil.

FRIZZY-HAIRED MAN
They were heavier than I thought
    Are you using more wood, or?

TREVOR
Metal

FRIZZY-HAIRED MAN
Oh my gosh
    I can't wait to see them
    This is so huge for me, Trevor

TREVOR
I know, baby

FRIZZY-HAIRED MAN
I mean the first time I
    Your opening at the Whitney
    I mean visceral and dark but um with

like this brutal intimacy
And so fucking beautiful
I'd never / seen anything

TREVOR
Okay why not drive back to campus
And yammer from the comfort of your dorm room

FRIZZY-HAIRED MAN
Oh
But just a second ago—

TREVOR
I changed my mind.
Go now.

FRIZZY-HAIRED MAN
Okay.
Um.
Need me to move anything else?

TREVOR
No thank you.

FRIZZY-HAIRED MAN
Okay.
(. . .)
Want a sandwich?
I can get you a sandwich

TREVOR
Good lord.

FRIZZY-HAIRED MAN
Could I just see one of them?
I won't take a picture or anything
See?
Here's my cell phone
I'll leave it / over there

TREVOR
You're about to make me into someone
    Who demonstrates incredibly bad romantic judgement

FRIZZY-HAIRED MAN
Well I helped you and everything
    And we did have pretty okay sex

TREVOR
Okay.
    a) No one sees these until they're done, not even my
husband
    b) Dignity, maybe? and
    c) Goodbye. Truly.

        The FRIZZY-HAIRED MAN *hesitates.*

FRIZZY-HAIRED MAN
(. . .) I fucked up.
    I peeked beneath the tarp

TREVOR
When?

FRIZZY-HAIRED MAN
Just for second
    I saw fur

TREVOR
Did you touch it?

FRIZZY-HAIRED MAN
Just for a second
    I couldn't help / myself

TREVOR
You touched it

FRIZZY-HAIRED MAN
Hardly, it was more like a

TREVOR
With the gloves on?

FRIZZY-HAIRED MAN
I took them off

TREVOR
Oh God

FRIZZY-HAIRED MAN
Just for a second

TREVOR
You idiot
     I said not to touch it

FRIZZY-HAIRED MAN
I know

TREVOR
I said "don't touch the art"

FRIZZY-HAIRED MAN
Nothing broke or

TREVOR
"hold the base by the straps"

FRIZZY-HAIRED MAN
The glue / was

TREVOR
Why did you touch it?

FRIZZY-HAIRED MAN
DRY, okay
     I didn't even SEE anything
     I just FELT it

TREVOR
Oh God

FRIZZY-HAIRED MAN
Trevor

TREVOR
Oh God

FRIZZY-HAIRED MAN
Trevor
    I'm sorry
    Please

TREVOR
(. . .)

FRIZZY-HAIRED MAN
What was the exact crime?
    Let me understand

TREVOR
Get out.

FRIZZY-HAIRED MAN
Trevor, I'm a—
    Please don't be mad
    I'm not like those freaks on the lawn with the camcorders
    I'm a fan Trevor but I'm not disgusting
    I'm not
    I'm not

> *Something beautiful and violent and dramatic happens to*
> TREVOR *here. The* FRIZZY-HAIRED MAN *does not*
> *hear or see her. Maybe he has disappeared, or is frozen.*

FBI MAN
Later that night
    I got a disturbing phone call

> *He gets a phone call. He answers it.*

FBI MAN *(cont.)*
Yello.
(. . .)
Uh-huhm.
(. . .)
Uh-huhm.
(. . .)
Uh-huhm.
(. . .)
Uh-huhm.
(. . .)
I'm there.

> *He hangs up.*

FBI MAN *(cont.)*
Hospital upstate.
   A matter of national security

   And so it begins.

• *This Could Be That*

> *During the following,* TREVOR *drives home from her studio. She wears special gloves.*

> *She hits several small animals along the way.* THUMP. THUMP. THUMP.

> *Each one she hits she stops and retrieves, with compassion and horror. Some of the animals are still alive.*

> *It is a dance; the Hit Animal Dance.*

> *It is funny.*

> *Meanwhile . . .*

The FBI MAN *stands next to a* DOCTOR.

They both stand over the corpse of the FRIZZY-HAIRED MAN.

The FBI MAN *reads from a small piece of paper in a plastic bag, which he handles with rubber gloves and tongs.*

The DOCTOR *is very, very nervous. He keeps looking over his shoulder.*

FBI MAN
"The Drive-bys
    The Ethnic Cleanse
    Checkpoint Fuckyou"

DOCTOR
Was in his back pocket
    Admitted this morning
    Dizziness, fatigue, fever
    We assumed it was a severe pleuropneumonic infection
    Dangerous but not enough to, um
    But then we found that paper
    So we did some tests
    By the time we figured it out, well
    (. . .)

    Rapid diagnostic testing is not widely available for this

FBI MAN
Uh-huhm

        He revolves around the body, examining it, like a dance.

DOCTOR
We are so glad you are here
    The disease is called "tularemia"
    "Rabbit disease"
    S-sm-smaller mammals act as reservoir hosts:

    prairie dogs, hares, muskrats, squirrels, voles
Humans can contract it several ways:
through ticks or flies or mosquitoes
or by handling the meat and skins of infected animals

FBI MAN
Uh-huhm

DOCTOR
Or um
    from food or water that has been contaminated
    or through the air
    if um, sprayed

FBI MAN
Uh-huhm

DOCTOR
Um
    Symptoms include:
    rapid onset
    sudden fever
    headaches
    muscle aches
    diarrhea
    joint pain
    dry cough
    progressive weakness
    It's one of the m-m-most infective bacteria known to m-m-man
    What, um, what

FBI MAN
It was used by the Russians during World War II
    Before that by the Japanese against Manchuria
    The U.S. developed strains of the disease in the '50s
    Part of their biological warfare program
    Terminated in the early '60s

When used as a weapon
The defense department classifies this
As a category 8 agent

DOCTOR
Wow.
   Um.

FBI MAN
The disease cannot be spread from person to person
   It infects through mucous membranes, the gastrointestinal tract,
   the lungs
   the skin

DOCTOR
We have no vaccine
   Everyone is so paranoid around here
   We sent the receptionist home
   The nurses think we moved him to CPU

FBI MAN
Good

DOCTOR
This
   of course this could be a single incident
   like Austerlitz
   the little girl
   Um
   This could be that
   if it weren't for the note

> The FBI MAN *takes off his Ray-Bans and leans into the*
> FRIZZY-HAIRED MAN, *to inspect him more closely.*
>
> *We see he has a long scar across one eye.*
>
> *A beat.*

DOCTOR *(cont.)*

He was twenty-one.

He was a student.

> *The* FBI MAN *returns his glasses to his face and looks at the back of the letter.*

FBI MAN

"With affection,

Trevor"

> *The* DOCTOR *disappears.*
>
> *The* FBI MAN *is in a spotlight, thinking. A dramatic moment for him. Maybe music.*
>
> *He opens his cell phone. Dials a few numbers.*

FBI MAN *(cont.)* *(into the phone)*

It's time.

How soon can you get it to me?

Perfect.

(To audience.)

I won't lie

I'm at my best

When the fate of the nation is at hand

Domestic situations however are not my specialty

International was always my bag

> *He opens a trunk of costumes.*
>
> *He dons an exterminator's outfit, "Bugs B-Gone," and a cap.*

Like any good agent

I adapt.

Voila.

Upstate New York.

Mission?

Discover whether or not target is knowingly utilizing
A classified biological weapon
For the threat toward and/or destruction of human life

So I motored up to Albany
Got myself a shitty, heatless efficiency
The heart of the Hudson Valley
And readied myself for the ride

    Meanwhile . . .

• *Prune Cedarwood*

    WILLIAM, MELANIE, TREVOR, *and* RANDY *are all
seated at dinner.*

    MELANIE *is a little giddy and tipsy. She is dressed elegantly.*

    TREVOR *is unreadable, but slightly on edge.*

    RANDY *eats in complete silence. He wears headphones.*

WILLIAM *(sipping wine)*
Prune
  Cedarwood
  Um

MELANIE
As a rule I'm not a red wine person but *this*

WILLIAM
The fellow recommended it /
  A little oaky, but

MELANIE
Mmmmm
  Okay
  Should we toast?

WILLIAM
To . . .

MELANIE
Trevor's new series?

TREVOR
Well that's swell of you Melanie
    But how can you toast to something you can't possibly grasp?

    (A slight beat.)

Having not seen it, of course.

MELANIE
Oh I know!
    To the first of many neighborly dinners!
    Thank you for having me, Trevor

TREVOR
Well you just kind of stopped by—

MELANIE
But you didn't have to let me in!

TREVOR
That is absolutely true.
    Cheers.

        They drink. The doorbell rings.

WILLIAM
Well gosh, now who could that be?

        TREVOR *gets it. It's the* FBI MAN *in his exterminator's outfit.*

TREVOR
Exterminator

FBI MAN
Keep eating
    I'll find my way around

No one looks at him.

He winks theatrically at us, then begins to inspect the house. He surreptitiously scrutinizes door hinges and vents.

MELANIE
Do you have vermin?

TREVOR
Just bugs
   Flies mostly.

WILLIAM
'Tis the season!
   Right?

TREVOR
My studio in the woods is filled with 'em
   They buzz around in circles like drunken pilots
   They know they're supposed to be dying
   Their bodies tell them so
   But it's not cold enough to knock them out
   So they kind of just flail around in a hazy purgatorio
   until their engines peter out
   Pretty soon my windowsill will be covered
   in a writhing pile of half-dead insects.

      MELANIE *finally notices* RANDY.

MELANIE
He certainly does enjoy his forks!
   (. . .)
   Ohhhh!
   A lyric just popped into my head.

Red redwiiiiiiine
   goes to my heeeeaaaad
   makes me forget that I'm

No no wait it goes:
Red redwiiiiiiine
stay close to me
don't let me be alone
Just mrahmrahngarahnga
And then there's a rap, I can't remember

Didn't you two used to make wine?
When Trevor first moved in?
(*To Trevor.*)
I remember you on your knees picking grapes outside
You were so young!
I asked what you what you were doing
You said "we're making wine"
But my brain heard "we're making love"
I was so ashamed—

WILLIAM (*suddenly remembering*)
Ah!
(*Rapping.*)
Red red wine you mek me feel so fine
You keep me rockin' all of the time

MELANIE (*delighted*)
Yes!

RANDY
Dad.

WILLIAM (*feeling a little foolish but going for it*)
Red red wine you mek me
    feel so grand
    I feel a million dollar when yajusin ma 'and

MELANIE
It's like a code!
    Keep going!

WILLIAM *(uncertain)*
Red red wine you mek me feel so sad
    Any time I see ya go it mek me feel bad

RANDY
Dad! I'm sharpening.

WILLIAM *(uncertain)*
Red red wine you mek me feel so fine
    Monkey back and moosaban a sweet ep line

MELANIE
WHAT?!

WILLIAM *(getting into it)*
Red red wine you give me oleeba-zing
    Oleeba-zing mek me do me own ting

MELANIE *(applauding)*
Yay!

WILLIAM
I'm sweating!

MELANIE
That was AMA / ZING

WILLIAM *(out of breath)*
We used to
    in college
    we'd play it over and over
    ah

MELANIE
Do you need some / water?

WILLIAM
I have the spins
    I'm okay

MELANIE *pours him some water.*

They all freeze.

Spotlight on the FBI MAN.

FBI MAN
Indulge me a moment.

> *He removes a tiny platinum box from his jacket pocket and smiles broadly.*
>
> *He opens the lid and carefully dips his pinkie into the box. He shows us something practically invisible on the tip of his finger.*

FBI MAN *(cont.)*
See this?

> *He walks into the audience. He confides in us. He whispers to us, cajoles us. Flirts.*

FBI MA *(cont.)*
Too small?
   Could be nothing, even?
   A grain of sand, a flake of paprika?
   A freckle?
   Pinprick from a tailoring misadventure?
   Ball-point pen mark?
   Insect dropping?
   Rat ovum?
   I could go on . . .

Well it isn't nothing
Not by a long shot
What you don't see here
Is a two-hundred-MILLION-dollar piece of surveillance
equipment

> *He scrutinizes his pinkie.*

FBI MAN *(cont.)*

Quadruple the signal-to-noise ratio and lux sensitivity of any previous machine close to its class
double the TVL and an optional ten thousand frames per second
thermal/infrared sensor fusion
multi-spectral nighttime imaging
360-degree non-angular field of view
rapid scan frequency
an UNLIMITED operation temperature—records data whether
you're at the North Pole or the gates of hell
half-mile operating distance
AND
98 percent accurate color reproduction

You know how many of these exist in the world?
You're looking at it
Sui generis.
Version one-point-zero.
Classified top secret hush-hush sub-rosa.

You know who they give this to?
No one.
It's never been used.
Tested only twice by the husband-wife team who developed it
Stowed in a platinum box in a crystal drawer in a steel vault in
an iron bunker
Dug a hundred miles down into the deep dark molten heart of
the earth
Where it was kept for precisely twenty weeks
After which time it was removed
And placed directly into my care.
Three hours ago.

   He places it carefully into the platinum box.

FBI MAN *(cont.)*

Why give it to *me*, you ask?
     I seem like an ordinary fellow.
     Hygienic but not suspiciously so
     Decent taste in footwear
     Marginally fit on a good day
     A sheen of competence akin to a mid-level executive

     I am not an opera
     I am not a threat
     I'm a block of clay-shaped clay
     I could even be you

     So.

     Why is it *me* holding this tiny precious box?
     The simple answer?
     Because I'm a patriot.

> *He drops his trousers. Beneath, he wears American flag boxer*
> *shorts.*

FBI MAN *(cont.)*

I realize I have not given myself a proper introduction.
     I'll do so via an oblique anecdote

     These under-wears were a gift from a lady friend
     Who, it turns out, was too much lady
     And not enough friend.

     One pair from a set of five.
     On the day she bought them
     She had gotten her hair permed
     She asked me to smell it
     I did
     pressed my face into her new curls
     the chemicals burned my eyes, nose, and throat
     I stayed there for a very long time

Burning
Because my loyalty to her was unwavering and bottomless
And the pain was but a small consequence.
(*A beat.*)
Precisely forty-seven weeks after the perm
I was called away for my job
Far away

When I returned, I was a few parts short
a fingernail
a toe
(*He removes his glasses.*)
an eye.
(*A beat.*)
I told my lady friend how I had spent my time away
But ladies don't like to hear such things
Ladies prefer to imagine their sojourning mates, oh,
doused in sunshine
sipping fruity drinks . . .

Not suspended from ceilings
beaten with chains
shocked with batons
or injected with drugs.

> *He pulls up his trousers.*

FBI MAN *(cont.)*
My position often requires long bouts of reflection
Which, at this point, lead me to two conclusions:

One:
As unwaveringly loyal as I was to my lady friend
I am precisely five hundred times more loyal to my job.

And two:
(*He places his glasses back onto his head.*)
I am bottomless.

He retrieves the tiny box again and peeks inside.

FBI MAN *(cont.)*
Did I mention this is waterproof?

The scene unfreezes and the **FBI MAN** *continues to work.*

The **FBI MAN** *addresses the room.*

FBI MAN *(cont.)*
Critters like hinges and ducts
  Warm places
  You got an animal, animals?
  Rodents, rabbits, prairie dogs? Voles?

WILLIAM
No.

MELANIE
Unless you count the ones in Trevor's Art Project
But they're all dead. Maybe they don't count?
I don't know what I'm talking about.

FBI MAN
All right.

MELANIE
I was thinking about going on the President's hike
  Or maybe the trolley museum
  We could pick apples

WILLIAM
Trevor's allergic to apples

MELANIE
REALLY???

MELANIE	**WILLIAM**
Wow.	Yes.
Wow.	Her throat constricts
Constricts?	

TREVOR
Imagine you're standing at the top of a steep hill
    Wearing a pretty scarf
    One end of the scarf is tied to a tractor in neutral
    The other end is being pulled by someone who doesn't like you.
    That's what it feels like.

MELANIE
(. . .) And the film festival!
    We need to get tickets early
    This controversial movie about child prostitution in Cambodia
    I'm not really interested but it sounds like something you might
    like

TREVOR
Well Melanie
    It's been a real pleasure
    I'm so happy you stopped by
    You are a stunning conversationalist
    And have flawless skin

MELANIE
You're leaving?

TREVOR
I need to get back to work

MELANIE
I brought blueberry crumble!
    I made / it!

TREVOR
Goodnight everyone
    Don't need me for a few hours

MELANIE
Okay.
    We'll save you a piece

TREVOR

Thank you

> TREVOR *exits. We see her in her studio, working, fretting.*

> *An odd beat.*

WILLIAM

Hey Randy.

How's Dr. Fredrick working out?

(*To* MELANIE.)

He's the highest rated adolescent therapist in the count . . .

> RANDY *exits, to his room, where he fight-dances.*

> *A beat as* MELANIE *and* WILLIAM *eat.*

WILLIAM *(cont.)*

Why did you come over, Melanie?

MELANIE

Crumble.

(. . .)

I wanted to get to know her a little better

WILLIAM

Why?

MELANIE

What do you mean, why? She's Trevor Pratt.

> *A beat.*

Do the dead animals bother you, William?

> *A small beat.*

WILLIAM

Of course not.

> WILLIAM *freezes.*

> *The* FBI MAN *pulls out a much-folded piece of paper from his wallet.*

FBI MAN *(reads)*
"Dear You.

Hi. This is an asignment"—one *s*—"from Mrs. Katzler's
eighth-grade comp class. Otherwise I wouldn't be doing it.

"You're now forty. You are probably married and divorced and
married again. You have a dog and a cat and a kid from each
marriage, and they all hate you. You like your wife fine but she
doesn't hump you anymore. You stopped smoking maybe, or
you have a stash in your basement that you secretly." ?? "You
are not a millionaire. But you're a boss of something lame. I
think you drink. You having an affair with the secretary.

"You won't remember me, so here: I'm quiet. I'm taller than
the other kids. I smoke. I eat alone. I like Jennifer Schultz and
I touched her ass once. I have brown hair. I watch a lot of TV.

"Times up. Bye.
Love,
You."

> The FBI MAN *folds up the paper again and smiles at us.*

FBI MAN *(cont.)*
One of the myriad reasons I was hired for this job—"hired" being
the loosest of terms in a rogue operation—is my ability to spe-
lunk the deepest recesses of an individual's psyche. (*Gestures to
the folded paper.*)
I wrote this letter to myself at thirteen. I saved it not because I
have a special misty-eyed nostalgia for the myopia of youth, but
because I thought I might need to remind myself that I once
aspired to mediocrity.

And why do I invoke it now, you ask?

Exhibit A.
(*He gestures to the frozen* WILLIAM.)

> *Spotlight on the frozen* WILLIAM.

FBI MAN *(cont.)*
William Whiting
Forty-four
Art historian
Sweats a lot
Has a fondness for cardigans
Never learned to swim
Was not in the car when his first wife died
Drinks tea with milk and sugar
Broke his nose once walking into a wall
Enjoys sad songs
Buys used books
Thinks it would have been "cool" to be a knight
Wishes his car were cleaner
Thinks his butt is squeezable
Hates cellular phones
(*Does an incredible, eerie impression of* WILLIAM.)
"A little oaky, but
Red red wine you mek me feel so fine
Trevor's allergic to apples
Trevor's allergic to apples"

· *It's on the Midterm*

> WILLIAM *appears at a podium, lecturing.*
>
> *The* FBI MAN *changes into college-student gear.*

WILLIAM
And I hope you dug last week's lecture,
"Vito Acconci and the Aesthetics of Contemporary Narcissism."
It's on the midterm!
Okey dokey smokies
Today we're gonna hit two controversial and "killer" artists

Guillermo Vargas and Trevor Pratt.
(. . .)

Guillermo Vargas
Costa Rican fella
Famous for tying a sick dog to a gallery wall
and allowing it to starve
Yikes, right?

Some say the dog was fed in off-hours
Others say it scurried off in the night
But Vargas claimed it died from neglect
No one knows the truth, oooooh
But the *point* was to expose hypocrisy
Vargas accused those who expressed outrage at the dog's treatment
of ignoring the same starving dog in the street
(. . .)

Question:
If we knew the dog had survived
would it change the way we feel about the work?

Which brings us to my former student
Trevor Pratt

As many of you know, Trevor and I
(. . .)

I am Pratt's legal partner
heretofore to be referred to in the third person

Pratt's exhibit *Impact* eight years ago
for which she acquired massive notoriety overnight

> WILLIAM *gestures to a series of slides as he talks: of a car accident, and maybe life-sized photos hanging in a gallery, along with a blowup of a police report and some other related documents. They are beautiful. Vivid colors. Blood.*

WILLIAM *(cont.)*
Photographs of a dead woman
    Killed in a head-on collision
    Priorly related to Pratt's partner by marriage
    Pratt enlarged the images
    And hung them

       Photo of a woman's body on asphalt. She looks like roadkill.

WILLIAM *(cont.)*
Where did she find them?
    On a shelf in the closet of her professor's bedroom
    (. . .)

       The FBI MAN *dons a baseball cap, a backpack, and a slouch.*

       He raises his hand to ask a question.

WILLIAM *(cont.)*
Yes, in the front?

FBI MAN
Like, her professor gave her permission to use these photos
    Why?

WILLIAM
Ah.
    Excellent question
    Was it an act of say, public mourning?
    A poor decision in the throes of grief?
    A fascination with the ethical implications?

    Why not let us consider the larger question:
    If we did not know the relationship of the artist to the subject
    would we still feel the emotional impact of the work?

    I address this in my new book, actually.
    (. . .)

*   *   *

which will be in stores

(. . .)

at some point.

> *The* FBI MAN *raises his hand again.*

WILLIAM *(cont.)*
Ah, yes?

FBI MAN
Like, do you think he regrets the decision?

WILLIAM
We can only speculate upon how he feels . . .
  Although I imagine he . . .
  (. . .)

  Picture the kind of man
  who butters toast every day
  married to a woman
  who butters toast every day
  Two toast butterers
  sitting in a butter-colored kitchen
  breathing together
  for fifteen years.

  Then
  one toast butterer
  gone
  the other . . . listless, shell-shocked . . .

> *A long beat. The* FBI MAN *changes this scene with his eye . . .*
> *lights? Music????*

> WILLIAM *crunches into himself.*

WILLIAM *(cont.)*
And THEN
> a lanky feral creature reaches into the wreckage to touch him
> Her hands get sliced by the shards
> but she doesn't flinch
> She isn't afraid of bleeding
> or even of pain
> She is fearless
>
> because she's the blade, you see
> The blade fears nothing
> it only cuts
>
> I'd never been that close to a cutting-person
> For me it was
> *she* was . . .
> catechismic
>
> I realized I could never butter toast again
> I could only be cut.

> *Sound stops. Lights normal.*

> *We're back in the classroom.*

WILLIAM *(cont.)* *(straightens)*
Um.
> Theoretically speaking.

> *The FBI MAN raises his hand again.*

WILLIAM *(cont.)*
Yes?

FBI MAN
Is she working on anything right now?

WILLIAM
I will leave that to her people to divulge

FBI MAN
Aren't you her people?

> *A beat.*

• *Thinking*

> The FBI MAN *is alone in his studio. Crappy smelly bed.*
> *Jammies. Gross unwashed coffee mug. Flickering bare bulb.*
>
> *He's thinking.*

FBI MAN
I'm just thinking.
(*A beat. He drinks from his coffee mug.*)
    This coffee has been sitting here for two days.
    I could make a fresh pot
    But I won't
    I prefer stale bitter cold
    I want to taste the rot
    It helps me think

What kind of woman
    I mean
    It's just
    (. . .)

You know?

I would say it's despicable
    But I'm not here to judge
    I'm here to probe, to sift, to root
    to bore

You know I didn't even know she was famous
    Until I googled her name.

*   *   *

I've been out of the loop.

However.
I'm no stranger to the capriciousness of the female mind.
>   My mother was a beauty queen
>   Miss University of Florida
>   I never saw her without makeup
>   Not even when she was drunk on the kitchen floor
>   lying in the lap of someone who was not my father
>   while my brother and I cleaned up their vomit . . .
(*A long long beat.*)
What was I saying?

>   *The* FBI MAN *thinks, drinks more bad coffee, then turns on his monitors to watch the house.*
>
>   *He watches an empty room for a little while. Music . . . We see his intense loneliness. Maybe he clips his toenails. Maybe he puts on lotion from a little blue jar. Maybe he does some crunches, some yoga stretches. It is a dance—the Sad Man Alone dance.*
>
>   *Suddenly:* TREVOR'*s face appears on the screen.*

TREVOR
Hello?
>   Exterminator?
>   Did you put a teeny tiny camera in my house?
>   A teeny tiny camera to watch what I'm doing?
>   Are you watching me right now?

>   *The* FBI MAN *stops breathing a moment.*

TREVOR (cont.)
I'm used to it
>   All eyes on me
>   I thrive on it

I'm a fucking narcissist after all
I have an inflated sense of self-worth
But somehow I feel invisible anyway
You know that feeling?

FBI MAN
I do

TREVOR
You have an inflated sense of my worth too
   Otherwise you wouldn't be watching me right now
   eating cereal
   scratching my ass
   getting drunk
   peeing
   Let me know if I get boring

FBI MAN
I make no promises

TREVOR
I need to go now
   I need to work

   Will you be here when I come back?

FBI MAN
Yes

TREVOR
Good.
Though I suppose you should know
   If you're looking for the hornet's nest
   you won't find it here

         She exits.

FBI MAN
Intriguing . . .

I suppose she wants me to follow her.
I don't "follow."
I lead.

> *The* FBI MAN *tries to sleep. Restless.*

> *Somewhere, elsewhere,* TREVOR *is working, watching TV.*

TV ANNOUNCER
And in local news
   A student has died in the Berkshires this week
   Twenty-one-year-old Benjamin Fizz
   Apparently he contracted the same rare bacterial disease
   Which claimed the life of young Callie Stewart.

> *Photo of the* FRIZZY-HAIRED MAN *somewhere, looking goofy.*

No need to panic, Berkshire residents.
But please stay out of the woods
   And away from the squirrels
   And do not touch your pets without gloves
   And do not go hiking
   Or fishing
   Or swimming
   Or hunting
   Or birding
   Or leaf-peeping
   And do not play outdoor sports
   And do not mow your lawn
   Or trim your bushes
   Or garden
   Or weed-whack
   Or rake
   Or hoe
   Until further notice

Thank you.

TREVOR *panics.*

TREVOR
I am fucked.
I am fucked.
I am fucked.
I am fucked.
I am fucked.

> *Then: the family appears for breakfast in the surveillance camera. The* FBI MAN *wakes up and watches.*

· *They Fed Me Veggie Booty*

> WILLIAM *and* RANDY *sit at the table eating cornflakes along with an assortment of breakfast items.*

> WILLIAM *wears pajamas and reads the paper.*

> RANDY *retrieves a briefcase and opens it. Inside is a fork collection. He considers his choices, then reaches for a tiny shrimp fork. He spears some sausages with it.*

Ding-dong.

> WILLIAM *answers.*

> MELANIE *enters wearing a fine-looking tracksuit and carrying two small sacks of coffee grounds.*

MELANIE
Morning, starshines!

WILLIAM
Melanie—

MELANIE
Did you notice the roads are so empty the past few days?

WILLIAM

It's the rabbit scare.

MELANIE

Oh.

Good thing I don't pay attention to *that* fluff! People get so worked
up over nothing, don't they?

(. . .)

So.

I was going for my morning walk and guess what I found?

A coffee roaster right next to the library!

It's new!

Isn't that FABULOUS?

I don't drink coffee but I know you and Trevor . . .

Oh!

Is she sleeping?

> TREVOR *walks in wearing her lab coat.*

TREVOR

Ah, Melanie, it's you

For a second I thought I was hearing
the sound of a large inflatable latex raft
being squeezed through a tiny metal hole

MELANIE

(. . .)

So!

I know it's early

I was just passing by on my walk

I brought over some beans.

I hope you have a grinder!

May I?

> MELANIE *disappears into the kitchen.*

> TREVOR *pours herself a bowl of cornflakes and sits.*

Coffee grinding is heard. It hurts the FBI MAN'*s ears.*

MELANIE *emerges again.*

MELANIE *(cont.)*
Well!
   You're all ground up.
   That's it I guess.
   (. . .)

TREVOR
Would you like to stay for breakfast?

MELANIE
Oh no no no no
   I was in the middle of my walk.
   Eating defeats the purpose!
   But maybe we could have tea soon?
   Or pizza?
   I don't really eat pizza
   Or sandwiches?
   Hundreds of options.
   I mean we've been neighbors for so long
   Let's start being neighborly!
   Right William?

     A beat.

WILLIAM
Thanks for the coffee Melanie
   Very thoughtful

     A beat.

MELANIE
Anyhoo.
   Have a good morning!

     She exits.

TREVOR

Think she's got an agenda knocking around that noggin or is it all impulse?

WILLIAM

Who knows. (*A small beat.*) You never came to bed

TREVOR

Sorry
   I'm in hot pursuit

WILLIAM

That's cool, that's cool.
   (. . .)

   You sure there's nothing else?

TREVOR

Yeah, why?

WILLIAM

Dunno.
   You seem a little
   (. . .)

TREVOR

Um.

WILLIAM

Everything OK?

TREVOR

Yeah.
   No.

WILLIAM

What is it?

TREVOR

Nothing.
   Just some re-jiggering

WILLIAM
With the piece?

TREVOR
Yeah.
    It's nothing.

WILLIAM
You sure?
    Wanna talk it out?

TREVOR
I don't really know how, to be honest

WILLIAM
Just ramble.
    I'll keep up

TREVOR
Okay, so.
    There's an element to it
    A very delicate, um
    that um
    has the potential to get me into a lot of trouble

WILLIAM
With who?
    The police?

FBI MAN
Or with me . . .

TREVOR
Um I don't know maybe

WILLIAM
Thrilling!
    And controversial!
    Oh! Is this about all the disease hysteria?

Are you addressing the cultural aggregation of paranoia
in western consciousness?
Sorry I'll shut up.
Continue.

TREVOR
So my use of this "controversial" element
    May or may not have been ah.
    Leaked.

WILLIAM
So you're saying
    you built in an ideological trip wire
    and it got tripped
    so its function has been prematurely fulfilled

TREVOR
Yeah.

WILLIAM
Are you in any trouble?

TREVOR
I don't know yet.

WILLIAM
Hmm.
    Well
    (. . .)

    Could I just say something here?
    Without knowing the details?
    Maybe it's not about the piece itself, then
    Maybe it's about the *context*.

TREVOR
Huh?

WILLIAM
The *event* of the piece exists in the past tense, right?
    So now it's a conversation about what was *intended*
    rather than what it *is*
    We're talking about *meaning* versus *being*
    It's performative almost

        TREVOR *blinks uncomprehendingly.* WILLIAM *becomes*
        increasingly excited, geeking out.

WILLIAM *(cont.)*
So
    The art IS the conversation
    Or rather
    The conversation is the art!
    A bridge to further thinking!
    Wow.
    How elegant is *that?*

TREVOR
I sorta wish I could drive an auger down your neck
    and crank it around

WILLIAM *(cont.)*
I'm sorry
    I know I'm not helpful
    (. . .)

    Just follow your instincts

RANDY
Are we gonna be famous again?

        A *small beat.*

WILLIAM
Randy.

RANDY
Like last time

WILLIAM
You were six

RANDY
I remember
    The lawn kids
    The camcorders
    They pitched tents
    They fed me Veggie Booty
    They took pictures of me
    They took pictures of everything

> WILLIAM *and* TREVOR *exchange nauseated glances.*

WILLIAM
It will be different this time

FBI MAN
Flashback: Fame Time.

> *Something immediate here—flashback to fame-time, or maybe just a whirlwind moment with music that demonstrates the hardiness and brutality of getting famous overnight—violent and out of control.*

WILLIAM
I need to shower
    Good luck, muffin.

> *He kisses* TREVOR.

WILLIAM *(cont.)*
And Randy.
    Kick ass at your audition

> *He gives* RANDY *an awkward thumbs-up.*

WILLIAM *(cont.)*
You're both superstars!

> *He exits.*

> TREVOR *is alone with* RANDY.

TREVOR *(kind)*
Listen.
  You need to be prepared.
  This isn't a joke.
  It *will* be different this time.
  (*A small beat.*)
  You're older now.
  I want to know you can handle it.

Tell me you can handle it.

> RANDY *explodes with some angry loud song, maybe*
> *"Gravedigger" by Pig Destroyer.*

RANDY *(sing-screaming)*
IN THIS TWO BEDROOM TOMB I'M SITTING ALL ALONE
  WITH THE TELEVISION STATIC AND REFRIGERATOR
  DROOOOOONE

  You don't scare me
  I broke into your studio
  Your stupid locks couldn't keep me out
  Some freaky shit, man
  Their eyes all bug

TREVOR
Did you touch anything?

RANDY
Sure
  Fondled all the girl rabbits
  Licked their little bunny twats.

He mimes licking bunny twats. Then laughs. Then waits for the
appropriate response from TREVOR. *Which he does not get.*

RANDY *(cont.)*
Doesn't that make you wanna hurl?

TREVOR
Yes, Randy.
    I want to hurl.

RANDY
Heh.

TREVOR
Let me ask you something.
    How badly do you want to be famous?

RANDY
Enough to eat rabbit pussy

TREVOR
Enough to die?

        A small beat.

RANDY
The fuck does that mean?

TREVOR
Just a question—

RANDY
Die?
    Like—

TREVOR *(carefully, touch of malice)*
Because if you touched those animals
    you're already dead.
    But you're going to be more famous
    than you could ever imagine.

RANDY *is slightly terrified.*

RANDY
I—

TREVOR
Did
   you
   touch
   them?

TREVOR *and* RANDY *are quiet a moment. All we hear is the crunching of the* FBI MAN's *popcorn.*

RANDY
No.

TREVOR
What did you do?

RANDY
I looked through the window.

TREVOR
Say it again.

RANDY
I looked through the window.

TREVOR
Say it again.

RANDY
I looked through the window.

A beat.

I didn't look through the window.
I didn't do anything.

He is about to cry.

TREVOR *(cont.)*
Okay.
>You did very well.
>You're a good little boy.
>You've earned a treat.
>I'll buy you some chocolate.
>Would you like that?

>>RANDY *nods.*

TREVOR *(cont.)*
Okay.
Have another cornflake.

>*They vanish.*

FBI MAN
Wow!
>She's so mean!!
>Ha!
>It's nuts!
>But is she mean enough to kill?

>>*Time passes. Perhaps we see more of the Sad Man Alone dance.*

>>*Then.* TREVOR *appears on screen again. She packs weed into a little bong.*

TREVOR
Yo, exterminator.
>Wanna hit?

FBI MAN
You smoke grass.
>I might have guessed.

TREVOR
Stole it from Randy's closet
>He keeps it stashed in a little pencil case

But never uses it
He's a good kid
Mostly

Don't tell William I got high without him
He hates that.

>   *She takes a hit.* FBI MAN *leers.*

FBI MAN
A dopehead, a thief, a terrorist AND a liar.
Watch the evils mount.

>   *To the audience.*

Have I told you I have exceptional instincts?
I'm a divining rod for the morally bankrupt
Back in training they called me "Dognose"
Something to do with sniffing out corruption I suppose
They didn't like me

I wasn't there to win friends
I was there to destroy enemies
I'm a patriot goddamn it.

TREVOR
Can I tell you something?

This might be strange
I'm not afraid of dying

I'm afraid of . . .

I'm afraid of being anesthetized
by blasphemies of the flesh

FBI MAN
Anesthetized—

TREVOR
I think about it a lot.

Sometimes?
When I've been watching those channels?

You know the channels
The ones with the machetes
And the bombs
And the guerrila fighters
And the severed limbs

My chin gets all tingly
And I think, "Fuck!
It's happening!
I'm *numbing*."

And then I'm just like everyone else out there
The non-feelers
The ones who pass by a starving dog
And keep on walking

And then I think
Maybe that's okay
Maybe it isn't a crime to make oneself numb
To that kind of extremity
We're all human
We all have thresholds

And that's the exact moment
I want to kill myself.

> *A beat. She laughs.*

I haven't been fucked in a while. Not well anyway.
Maybe that's my problem.

> *She suddenly becomes deadly serious.*

I never meant to hurt him.

FBI MAN
Who?

TREVOR
He was so young.
I thought he wouldn't get it
The fuck do I know about kids
When he came home that day
After seeing the—

I looked into his eyes
His pupils were tiny
He kept saying
"That wasn't her.
That wasn't her."

He let me hold him.
He never let me hold him.

     A beat.

I wonder why you haven't come for me yet
Maybe 'cause you like to watch

Or maybe you're like a python
Waiting to strike

FBI MAN
A python . . .

TREVOR
Or maybe you're just waiting to see
How far I'll go

I can tell you:

     She holds up a syringe.

All the way.

     A long beat. Maybe FBI MAN *is sweating.*

TREVOR *(a whisper)*
Come with me.

FBI MAN
Where are we going?
I need answers—

TREVOR
Bye.

>   *She exits.* FBI MAN *is stunned a moment.* HE *shakes it off.*

FBI MAN
"All the way."
What could that mean?

>   *He thinks. He does other things.*

>   RANDY *appears somewhere, still in his chicken leg, preparing for his audition.*

That poor little mutant.

>   *Then, to the audience.*

I was famous once.
   When I was eleven years old
   Our neighbor shot his wife
   I stood behind the crime scene tape
   Local news rushed over
   Woman with a microphone asked what I thought
   (. . .)

   What *I* thought?
   No one had ever asked me that
   I said the wife deserved it
   They aired it
   My mother was so proud

>   *   *   *

Years later
   after my brother's suicide
   the cameras came to *my* house

I smiled for them

     Spotlight on RANDY.

FBI MAN *(cont.)*
Randy Whiting
   Fourteen
   No girlfriend
   Has a fork collection
   Could eat Doritos every meal
   Lost his virginity last year
   Collects vampire comics
   Mother died when he was six
   Likes to be clean
   Ate a live beetle on a dare
   Wishes his life were digital
   Can't grow a mustache
   Loves pizza bagels
   Allergic to penicillin
   Wishes he were famous

     RANDY *starts dancing as before.*

     The FBI MAN *dresses as a chicken nugget.*

RANDY
You no longer have to deny your chicken cravings
   just because they strike at night
   We now have more than 750 locations throughout the country
   offering a special Late Night menu
   Satisfy those cravings with favorites like
   Lil' Snackers, Crispy Strips, Pop-Its—

He stops dancing.

A beat.

RANDY	FBI MAN
Look at me.	Look at me.
Look at me.	Look at me.
Look at me.	Look at me.
Look at me.	Look at me.

• What Are You Anyway?

RANDY *is sitting in a chair wearing his chicken leg costume. He is chatting to the* FBI MAN, *who is still dressed as a chicken nugget.*

The FBI MAN *is sharing a bag of Doritos with* RANDY.

They are at an audition.

RANDY
Fuckin' people
   Thanks dude
   (*A long beat, with crunching.*)
   What are you anyway, dude?

FBI MAN
A nugget

RANDY
Oh. I thought you were a thigh.
   (*A long beat, with crunching.*)
   I'm sweating balls
   This is a shit gig
   Fuckin' costume smells like cheese dick

   The FBI MAN *stares at* RANDY *strangely.*

RANDY *(cont.)*
You wanna fuck me or sumpthin'?

FBI MAN
You look so friggin' familiar, dawg
　　Can't figure it out

RANDY
What about now?
　　(*Sudden screaming. And violent dancing.*)
　　MOVE YOUR BODY TO THE PUNK BEAT
　　WHILE POUNDING YOUR OPPONENTS
　　TO A BLOODY PULP

　　THIS GRUESOME DANCE GAME COMBINES
　　STREET-STYLE FIGHTING WITH
　　HARDCORE MUSIC
　　FOR INTENSE COMPETITION
　　AND BLOODSHED LIKE YOU'VE NEVER SEEN

FBI MAN
Holy shit!
　　That was you!
　　The "fan-mercial"

RANDY
Two hundred thousand hits, bro
　　I was like a YouTube phenomenon

FBI MAN
You wore bike chains
　　black eyeliner
　　spiked hair
　　And you had those contact lenses
　　Gave you crazy wolf eyes

RANDY	FBI MAN
OOOOOOWWWWW	OOOOOOWWWWW
WWWWWWWWW!	WWWWWWWWW!

They laugh and fist-bump.

RANDY *(cont.)*
It's a dope fuckin' game, man
   Ever play?

FBI MAN
Naw

RANDY
This gangster called Dwight
   He's a MENACE, right
   He owns everything
   Total terrorist
   And there's this chick, Ruby Sue
   She's a cage dancer at this punk club
   Basically he makes her his slave
   She's like chained to the bar
   And so it's your job to out-dance everyone in the club
   But also, you're beating the shit out of them
   Like crunk street fighting?
   (Shows a move.)
   Right?
   Different moves get different points
   (Shows another move.)
   Fiddy!

RANDY
Sucka!

RANDY *(shows another move)*
A hundy!

RANDY
Taste it! Taste it!

> RANDY *shows another move. And another. It is horribly violent.*

RANDY

And there's blood everywhere
   Like the walls are drenched
   And your eyeball is hanging by its optic nerve
   And then you get to Dwight
   and you have to slice him from chin to nuts
   And once you've done that
   you have the option of eating his heart

FBI MAN

Tight, tight.
   Sounds fucking rad

RANDY

I had to stop playing it at home
   My stepmom has a thing about violence or whatever

FBI MAN

She's pretty whack?

RANDY

Um
   Dunno
   She's got issues

FBI MAN

Who doesn't

RANDY

Right?
   You probably know her
   She's like, actual world-famous

FBI MAN

Dude, who is she?

RANDY

Trevor Pratt

FBI MAN
I know that name, bro . . .

RANDY
She's an artist

FBI MAN
Heeey
   Didn't she have those pix of the car accident?
   With the dead chick?

> *A small beat.*

RANDY
Yeah

FBI MAN
Oh snap!
   Dude, wasn't that your mom?

> *A beat.*

RANDY
I wasn't supposed to see them
   But they were like, everywhere
   In the supermarket magazines
   On TV

> *The* **FBI MAN** *changes the scene with his eye . . .*

RANDY *(cont.)*
I shat the bed
   I scratched the skin off my cheeks
   They took my TV
   They made me bite a stick

FBI MAN
Why would your stepmom do that to you?

> *RANDY shrugs. He gets edgy, uncomfortable.*

FBI MAN
Where does she work?

RANDY
In the woods somewhere.

FBI MAN
Where?

RANDY
Hey who are you man?
  Just some chicken thigh sitting here

FBI MAN
I'm a nugget, homes

RANDY
I don't have to tell you shit

FBI MAN
Just making conversation

RANDY
Whatever
  Fuck this gig, man
  I don't even need it
  We're gonna be famous again
  This time I'm not gonna fuckin cry in the corner
  This time IT WILL BE SAVAGE

Thanks for the Doritos

> RANDY *exits. Lights change back.*

> *The* FBI MAN *has a moment. He changes into his jammies again. He picks up the cold coffee from before. Music?*

> *The* FBI MAN *continues thinking, and drinking bad coffee.*

FBI MAN *(to audiences)*
Shat the bed

Bit a stick
(!!!)

Everything I learned about Trevor Pratt
turned my stomach one quarter turn more

> *Of course he is not revolted at all. Quite the opposite.*

> *He begins his nightly routine again, furiously.*

FBI MAN *(cont.)*
Lack of empathy
   total sociopath
   "the fuck do I know about kids"
   you're insane
   you didn't think showing a six-year-old
   pix of his mom as roadkill
   would turn him loopy?
   A biological weapon in the hands of someone like her
   (. . .)

(Brushes his teeth. Thinks.)
I need to get closer to her somehow
Peel back her rind
Slice into her pulp

But how?

Jumpcut. Two nights later. Trevor is driving to her studio.

> *Continues his nighttime grooming routine. Maybe he clips his toenails. Maybe he puts on lotion from a little blue jar. Maybe he does some crunches, some yoga stretches.*

> *He tries to go to sleep in his drafty apartment with a threadbare blanket. We again see his hardship. His loneliness.*

> *Simultaneously:*

• *Interlude: Trevor Drives from Her Studio*

> TREVOR *drives from her studio.*
>
> *She hits several small animals along the way.* THUMP.
> THUMP. THUMP.
>
> *Each one she hits she stops and retrieves. But the dance is
> different this time. Not as funny.*
>
> *Meanwhile, the* FBI MAN *cannot sleep. He turns the
> surveillance camera on once again, and watches.*

• *I Have Cobbler*

> MELANIE *is wandering around the house clutching a peach
> cobbler.*
>
> *The* FBI MAN *watches.*

MELANIE *(cheerful)*
Hello?

> Hello?
> Anyone?
> I have cobbler

> TREVOR *enters, gloves covered in blood.*

TREVOR
Excuse the blood
   I was flossing
   Cocoa Puff?

MELANIE
No thank you.

TREVOR *pours herself a bowl of Cocoa Puffs and munches the entire time* MELANIE *chats.*

MELANIE *(cont.)*
Goodness!
Well you've been a busy beaver haven't you!

Beaver
(???)

MELANIE *hands* TREVOR *the cobbler.*

TREVOR
Hey mind if I ask you a question?
What's with all this sloshing good will?

MELANIE
No reason!
It isn't even good.
The peaches weren't ripe
I ran out of sugar
I substituted cornstarch
I left the price tag on the crust
You can bring it to the barn later
I mean your studio
Ha!
I still think of it as a barn!
Well.
I'll put it here.
(. . .)

I'll just pop over later for the plate

FBI MAN
Where is the barn, Trevor?

MELANIE
Pop-over
(???)

A long beat. TREVOR *returns to her Cocoa Puffs.*

MELANIE *(cont.)*
So how are things?

TREVOR
Pretty good

MELANIE
When do you think you'll be done?

TREVOR
Soon

MELANIE
Exciting.

FBI MAN
Exciting indeed . . .

MELANIE
So!
> So your work!
> Dead animals.
> (. . .)
>
> Gosh.

>   *A beat.*

TREVOR
Do they bother you, Melanie?

>   *A long beat.* MELANIE *struggles.*

MELANIE
Be nice to have people around again
> The cameras, the snacks
> Never boring, that's for sure

Ha!
But.

TREVOR
You know, Melanie
I think you might be my ideal audience.

> *A beat.*

MELANIE
Really?
> Oh my god.
> Are you serious?
> Oh my God!
> I am so honored.
> So very—
> I'm having trouble finding the words
> (. . .)
> I'm calling it off with William

FBI MAN
WHAT?!

MELANIE
I'm deeply unsatisfied
> We don't communicate
> His mind drifts
> Sometimes when we make love
> He gives up in the middle
> (*A beat.*)
> You knew, right
> About him and me

TREVOR   FBI MAN
No.   No.

MELANIE
Oh.
> It was only a few times.
> Maybe seven.
> We only talked a little
> He talks more to me in his sleep than in life!
> Sometimes he lectures
> Sometimes he apologizes
> To who, right??

FBI MAN
Melanie.

MELANIE
You know before you came along
> We used to wave at each other
> Him walking his dog
> Me walking my cat
> Hello, good morning, beautiful weather
> Neighborly waving
> His wife too
> Hello good morning look at the leaves
> She looked so much like him

> Then you moved in
> And suddenly
> You were both on your knees with the grapes
> I didn't understand

> *(A beat.)*

TREVOR
Why are you telling me this?

MELANIE
I have no one to talk to
> I think about you a lot.

> So!

I'm ready
to be friends
What do you think?
Could we do that?

A long beat.

TREVOR
Hey Melanie
    Guess what?

MELANIE
What?

TREVOR
Go on!
    Guess!

MELANIE
What?
    I don't understand
    What am I guessing?

TREVOR
Just guess.
    Anything.

MELANIE
Okay.
    Give me a ballpark.

TREVOR
Guess what I think of you.

MELANIE
Oh!
    (. . .)

    Well I haven't a clue!

TREVOR
Don't even wanna try?

MELANIE
Well I suppose you think I'm cheerful?
    And I have clean hair?
    And you like my skin, you mentioned that the other day . . .

TREVOR
I think
    that you are
    a cunt.

> *Stunned silence. A long beat.*

> TREVOR *bursts into laughter. A relieved* MELANIE *follows*
> *suit. So does the* FBI MAN. *He changes into rustic gear.*

MELANIE *(laughing)*
My goodness!

TREVOR
The look on your face!
    You were all . . .

> TREVOR *mimics* MELANIE's *look.*

MELANIE
I *was!*
    I *was* all . . .

> MELANIE *mimics* TREVOR *mimicking* MELANIE's *look.*
> *The women laugh and laugh. Then they calm down.*

TREVOR
Go away now
    Get a haircut

MELANIE
Um

TREVOR
Buy a bright red belt
    Take a long clarifying walk

MELANIE
Okay
You know
    When everything blows over
    I really do think we could be actual friends

> TREVOR *moves to the door and opens it for* MELANIE.

TREVOR
Thanks for coming.

> MELANIE *is about to leave. She feels something odd, and turns back.*

MELANIE
Is something about to happen, Trevor?

> *They freeze.*

FBI MAN
Great question, Melanie.

    Something IS about to happen, yes
    What is it, Trevor?

    Me
    Infiltrating enemy lines
    Me
    The blood on your lab coat
    The disease on your fingers
    Me me me me

    I'm gonna climb into your world
    Snuggle up with your little "project"
    And get nice and cozy

I will be so fucking close
You won't know where you end and I begin

We will become the ouroboros
Me the head, you the tail

And I will eat you alive.
(. . .)

　　　TREVOR *disappears.*

FBI MAN
How you ask?

　Through your ideal audience

　Things just got personal.

　　　Spotlight on MELANIE.

FBI MAN *(cont.)*
Melanie Colander
　Thirty-seven
　Divorced
　No children
　Has a silk scarf collection
　Lives alone
　Pees with the door shut
　Loves jam
　Reads tabloids
　Takes a milk bath every Friday
　Hates mold
　Does not masturbate
　Is not a good listener
　(*Does an incredible, eerie impression of* MELANIE.)
　"Gosh this wine
　I have no one to talk to
　Dead animals
　Is something about to happen, Trevor?
　Is something about to happen, Trevor?"

• *Anyone Can Make Themself Happy*

> MELANIE *is on her knees in her garden, wearing gardening gear, a silk scarf, fussy shoes, and a bright new red belt.*

> *The* FBI MAN *approaches, wearing his outdoorsy gear.*

FBI MAN
Pardon me . . .
  I'm looking for Hill Road?

MELANIE
You're on it

FBI MAN
Oh
  I didn't see a sign

MELANIE
It's blocked by the big "L"
  This used to be a horse farm

FBI MAN
Sorry to bother you

MELANIE
No bother
  I'm just murdering shrubs

FBI MAN
Your hole isn't deep enough
  Dig about four times the width of the root ball

MELANIE
Gosh!
Are you a gardener?

FBI MAN
I dabble

MELANIE

You're like me!

   A dabbler!

   I love to dabble.

   You like to do nice things for yourself too, right?

FBI MAN

I do

MELANIE

I knew it!

   It's a type

   Like, yesterday?

   I accidentally watched the news

   and I woke up in such a state!

   So I went golfing by myself

   I got to the course and I took off my shoes

   and lay my putter down

   and then I walked on the green grass barefoot

FBI MAN

Ooooh.

MELANIE

Cool and soft like a thick pile rug

   I walked and walked

FBI MAN

Mmmmmm.

MELANIE

And the other day?

   I made a cobbler

   The peaches weren't ripe

   I ran out of sugar

   I substituted cornstarch

   I left the price tag on the crust

   I can't make desserts

I can't make anything really

But it was fun!!!

> MELANIE *zones a moment. She looks down at her bright red belt, touches it.*
>
> *Snaps back.*

MELANIE *(cont.)*
You know?
I think it's the small kindnesses one does for oneself that
(. . .)

It's my theory that I made up
Close out the ugliness
Close it out
Know what I mean?

FBI MAN
I do, I do

MELANIE
Because people, humans I mean
Well there's a lack of elegance
It's endemic

FBI MAN
Yes.

MELANIE
And overseas, the violence?
Well what the heck's wrong with innocence
for those of us who have the option
Which is anyone, really
ANYONE can make themself happy
So why not choose that
Why WALLOW?
I have a strict no-wallowing policy

FBI MAN
So smart.

MELANIE
This scarf is pure silk
    Jodie Foster is gay
    Are you married?

FBI MAN
Divorced

MELANIE
Me too!
    Well!
    Where are you from?

FBI MAN
Spencertown

MELANIE
What brings you over here?

FBI MAN
House for sale

MELANIE
Which one?

FBI MAN
425?

MELANIE
Oh.
    You must have the wrong Hill Road

FBI MAN
Google Maps, um

MELANIE
That house isn't for sale

FBI MAN
My Realtor—

MELANIE
Who is your Realtor?

FBI MAN
Missy . . . ah Missy . . .

MELANIE (*distant*)
Unless he put it on the market this morning, or . . .
    That's so strange
    He never mentioned

FBI MAN
I heard a famous artist lives there

MELANIE
Oh
She's not famous anymore
    Now she just scrapes dead animals off the side of the road
    Isn't that AWFUL?

FBI MAN
Why does she do that?

MELANIE
It's her art
    She keeps them in a barn
    She calls it her studio

FBI MAN
Is it nearby?

MELANIE
The barn?
    Not really
    It's pretty deep in the woods
    Lot of dark windy roads—

FBI MAN
Where?

MELANIE *(suddenly shy)*
Oh.
  It's private

FBI MAN
Could I
  could you
  forgive me
  I'm not normally
  But a famous . . .

MELANIE
She's working on something
  I don't think she likes to have visitors there

FBI MAN
Of course not
  Stupid of me
  I've taken enough of your time

MELANIE
Not at all

        A long beat. The FBI MAN *changes the scene somehow, with
        his thoughts, his eyes, his one bad eye . . . music?? Lights????*

MELANIE **(cont.)** *(dreamy)*
Sometimes?
  In the market?
  I stare at the packets of meat?
  The loose blood in the cellophane?
  And um

FBI MAN
Melanie

MELANIE

And yesterday I was driving at night
  I hit something
  I turned around to see if it was still alive
  It was a possum
  Scattered behind it was a handful of wet babies

          A long beat. Music off abruptly.

FBI MAN

Thank you so much for the info
  You're a lovely woman
  (*He kisses her hand gallantly.*)
  Flawless skin

          He hands her a card.

          Then he exits.

          She watches after him. Then freezes.

          The FBI MAN *turns to us. He smiles.*

FBI MAN *(cont.)*

Bingo.

          But then.

    That afternoon
    I got a disturbing phone call

          He gets a phone call. He answers it.

FBI MAN *(cont.)*

Yello.
  (. . .)
  Uh-huhm.
  (. . .)
  Uh-huhm.
  (. . .)

Uh-huhm.
(. . .)
Uh-huhm.
(. . .)
Evidence?
(*Hand on the mouthpiece, to us.*)

They're getting antsy
   (*Back on the phone.*)
   Well it's a delicate—
   (. . .)
   I don't want to rush into—
   (. . .)
   She's a very—
   (. . .)
   I don't have anything concrete yet—
   (. . .)
   Buh-bye.

         He hangs up. Miffed. Very angry.

FBI MAN *(cont.)*
They're giving me a week.
   A fucking *week* to determine malicious intent
   And or knowledgable use of a controlled substance
   For the purposes of blah blah blah.
   They don't understand at all.
   I hate that

   I did not take on this assignment
   for a hasty hacky bullcrappy—
   (!!!)
   I took it because I have questions
   about human nature
   about the desire to kill
   about myself

* * *

Is a measure of artfulness
too much to ask?

They don't understand the ineffable language of war

And this is war, my comrades.
A war of wills

> *He flips on the monitors to watch* TREVOR.

> *But the camera no longer shows the house.*

> *It has moved. It is dark.*

FBI MAN *(cont.)*
What the . . .
  (*He squints at the camera.*)
My monitor—

> *Lights brighten the screen.* TREVOR *appears on camera. In her studio. Smiling.*

TREVOR
Welcome.
  Figured I'd heat things up a bit.
  Hope you don't mind.

> *She turns the camera a bit. Patch of fur, Set of eyes.*

FBI MAN
Ooohh
  Now you're playing with fire, sweetheart

TREVOR
This is my *other* home
  Meet the gang
  Dieter, Alan, Benzy, Justin, Veronika
  I spend more time with these guys than I do with my real family
  Does that seem sick?

Well I am sick.
A little
more than a little
I'm not eating, not sleeping
I can't feel here, here, and here
My instincts are totally tweaked
I'm stuck
I'm stuck
And I don't have much time
(*To camera.*)
Or do I?
How much time do I have?

FBI MAN
Um . . .

TREVOR
Because this is driving me a little bonkers
    The not knowing
    Waiting for the angry knocking
    the dudes in hazmat suits
    helicopters, sirens

    I mean really
    what the fuck are you waiting for?
    This is a huge fucking deal
    A matter of national fucking security

FBI MAN
Whoa, whoa, whoa
    Slow down, game-changer—

TREVOR
I need help
    I don't know what I'm asking for
    I don't even know who I'm asking
    But I'm—

* * *

I have no one
Just you

Can you help me?

She freezes. A long beat.

FBI MAN
Help her
Help her

But what about the rules?

He smiles knowingly.

Know what happened last time I followed rules?

He flips up his eyepatch dramatically.

Adiós a mis ojos.

He flips it back down.

He dons a rain jacket.

I would discover what the moment required
From within the moment itself

Mini jumpcut. The next day. I had a date with destiny

He douses himself with a bucket of water.

· **Not Dead**

TREVOR*'s studio.*

Small light flicks on. MELANIE *and the* FBI MAN *enter. It is raining outside, they are damp, they shake out umbrellas.*

MELANIE *carries an open bottle of wine.*

MELANIE
Hee!

FBI MAN
Shhhhh . . .

MELANIE
Goodness
    Never broken into anything in my life!
    I feel WILD!!!

FBI MAN
Shhhhh!

MELANIE
You picked those locks like a pro

FBI MAN
I'm a contractor
    We get locked out of things a lot

MELANIE
Hee!
    This wine is making me,
    Whoooo!
    Okay now remember, if she comes by
    I'm here for my plate

FBI MAN
Thank you for bringing me here, Melanie
    You're a total doll

MELANIE
Oh, now—

FBI MAN
And so brave!

MELANIE
Oh stop.
> I'm really not brave
> I'm just drunk

FBI MAN
You know who you remind me of?
> Amelia Earhart

MELANIE
Shut up!

FBI MAN
You do!
> A fearless woman
> plunging herself into unknown territory
> Very very sexy . . .

> *The* FBI MAN *nibbles on* MELANIE's *scarfed neck. She squeals.*

MELANIE
Do I smell nice?
> It's a cinnamon spritz
> I wanted to smell homemade
> You still haven't told me what happened to your eye

FBI MAN
It's confidential

MELANIE
Man of mystery . . .
> Hee!
> Would you like a scarf?
> I brought extra to cover the odor

> MELANIE *giggles and takes out a scarf. She squirts a scent onto it.*

> *The* FBI MAN *takes it, holds it against his nose.*

MELANIE *(cont.)*
Let's not be here too long . . .

FBI MAN
All right
  Are you ready for lights, Amelia?

MELANIE
Oh my gosh oh my gosh
  YES!
  Do it do it!

> MELANIE *shields her mouth with her scarf.*

> *The* FBI MAN *turns on an overhead light.* MELANIE *gasps.*
> *Both look around at all the work, which is half uncovered.*

> *The* FBI MAN *is amazed.* MELANIE *is filled with horror.*

MELANIE *(cont.)*
I
  Goodness
  I

FBI MAN
My God
  It's beautiful

> *One of the animals twitches.* MELANIE *shrieks.*

MELANIE
AHHHHH!
  Not dead!
  Not dead!

> *She runs to the* FBI MAN's *arms, hysterical. He comforts her*
> *and speaks to the audience.*

> *Suddenly, the* FBI MAN *has a stunning, awful, grotesque, yet*
> *perfect idea.*

FBI MAN *(to MELANIE)*
It won't hurt you

MELANIE
Why would anyone—
    It doesn't make any—
    I mean they're living breathing—

FBI MAN
Calm down—

MELANIE
It's HORRIBLE!
    It's HORRIBLE!
    You can't
    You can't kill things!
    You can't kill things and call it art!

FBI MAN
Why not?
    The world does it
    We all kill things
    in the name of other things

MELANIE
I want to go home

FBI MAN
If you show you're frightened
    You lose your advantage
    Do you want her to win?

MELANIE
Win?
    Win what?
    I don't / under

FBI MAN
Climb into her mind

See what she's after
Know your enemy

MELANIE
She's not my / enemy

FBI MAN
With empathy comes knowledge, Melanie
I learned this as a contractor

The best way to truly *know* a person
is to *become* that person

MELANIE
Oh dear

FBI MAN
Don't shut down like "Melanie"
Open yourself like "Trevor"
It's your only way in

MELANIE
N-now?
I don't think I'm quite / prepared

FBI MAN
Now.
Open yourself

A beat.

MELANIE
Open.

FBI MAN
Brave.

MELANIE
Open brave.

> MELANIE *takes a long drink of wine.*
>
> *Then she faces the animals.*
>
> *She becomes trancelike.*

FBI MAN
What do you see?

MELANIE
Their eyes . . .

FBI MAN
What else . . .

> *Music, or sound, or noise begins to rise in the room, building. Or are the animals singing?*

MELANIE *(dreamy)*
I hit a possum the other day
  I dreamt I ate its babies

> *She is captivated. No going back.*

FBI MAN
If it moves you
  You should touch it

> MELANIE *is very close to one animal. The animal turns its head to* MELANIE *a little.*
>
> MELANIE *gasps a little.*
>
> *Her hand reaches out slowly.*
>
> MELANIE *touches the animal. Then strokes the animal.*
>
> *The* FBI MAN *flinches. But says nothing.*

MELANIE *(exhilarated, quiet)*
He's warm
  (. . .)
  Oh my gosh

She continues to stroke the animal.

The FBI MAN *lets her. Face wrinkled with nausea . . .*

Something happens to the FBI MAN. *Maybe* MELANIE
*freezes, lights and music shift to reveal some turning point, or
his inner turmoil at watching this. Or maybe not.*

The FBI MAN *bursts from the scene.*

· Was That Necessary?

During the following, TREVOR *drives to her studio. She
wears special gloves.*

She hits several small animals along the way. THUMP.
THUMP. THUMP.

Meanwhile . . .

The FBI MAN *is doing angry pushups or sit-ups, listening to
his iPod. He is very very sweaty, shouting to himself over his
tunes. Punishing himself.*

Unhinged a bit.

FBI MAN
But it's important to keep this in mind:
   Baseness may only occur
   When the regulating force
   Has become defunct
   And I am a vigorous self-regulator

I do this with a frothing conviction
Press my nose to my own feces
And scream "WAS THAT NECESSARY?"
And if the answer is no, well . . .

Who is accountable?
ME.

> *He smashes the iPod against his head.*

FBI MAN *(cont.)*
THE GOVERNMENT.
(Smashes again.)
A PATRIOT.
(Again.)
ME. ME. ME.

> *Again again again. Then he throws it across the room.*

> *A beat. He breathes, pulls himself together.*

FBI MAN *(cont.)*
It *was* necessary.
It was.
It was.

· *What's Missing*

> TREVOR *appears in her studio, working with a dying animal.*

> *The* FBI MAN *watches on the monitor.*

> *She is outfitted in a chemical hazard suit. She handles a chemical in a syringe extremely carefully.*

> *Only a few of the pieces are covered in tarps now.*

> *She works and works. She talks to the animal.*

TREVOR
Okay

This is gonna hurt like a motherfucker
Deep breaths
(*She injects a chemical into an animal. The animal squirms.*)
Shhhh
I'll sing you a song I've been working on
Yeah I wrote a song
It's a lullaby
It's called
"The Keeper of the Marvel"
(*She hums an intro. Then sings:*)
I'm the hmm hmm hmm—
(*Stops.*)
That's as far as I got.
(*The animal winces.*)
I know it's not much comfort right now
　　But try to remember:
　　You will be rewarded
　　when the doors are flung open

> *Then she is done.*

> *She moves this animal with the others.*

> *She evaluates all her work. The whole thing.*

> *She is frustrated.*

TREVOR *(cont.)*
Shoot fuck balls.

FBI MAN
What's missing?

> TREVOR *turns the TV on. War, violence. She pinches herself. She smacks herself in the face, pulls at it, etc. She's getting numb.*

> *She turns the TV off and paces a little.*

FBI MAN *(cont.)*
Blasphemies of the flesh . . .

> *Knock on the door.*

> TREVOR *removes her gloves and opens it.* MELANIE *is outside. She looks awful. She is coughing and hacking and shaking, and very weak.*

> *The* FBI MAN *watches.*

MELANIE
H-hello
  I came for my plate

TREVOR
Jesus
  Are you all right?

> MELANIE *stumbles into the studio. She wears sweats, heels, a scarf.*

MELANIE
Bronchitis
  I think
  It's not contagious
  Could I sit?

> MELANIE *slumps in a heap of coughing.* TREVOR *grabs a chair and steadies her in it.*

> *The* FBI MAN *watches.*

TREVOR
You look / terrible

MELANIE *(weakly)*
So
  How's William?
  How's he been?
  That's great

And Randy?
Oh, maybe next time
And you?
Almost done?
Wonderful
Apples, crazy!
My shoes?
On SALE
Computers
Pants
Fruit cups
Billiards
The animals
I wasn't expecting—
Their bodies were warm

TREVOR
Which / animals?

MELANIE
I was here
    Last night

TREVOR
You weren't here

MELANIE
I came for my plate

TREVOR
You couldn't have gotten in

MELANIE
He picked the locks for me

TREVOR
Who?

MELANIE
I didn't come for my plate.
   I came for um
   Um
   Um-um-um-um-um-um
   (. . .)
   Umpathy

> *Coughing fit.*

TREVOR
Lay down
   Over here

MELANIE *(weakening)*
Anyhoo
   You should—
   We all should—
   Have dinner, or
   (. . .)

> MELANIE *closes her eyes.*

> *A long long beat.*

MELANIE **(cont.)** *(quietly)*
Say something.

> TREVOR *opens her mouth to speak. War sounds.*

TV ANNOUNCER
A three-vehicle convoy
   was struck by a roadside bomb
   Eighty miles outside the Gaza Strip
   Seven Israelis were killed

> TREVOR *closes her mouth. She opens it. War sounds.*

TV ANNOUNCER **(cont.)**
Then a bomb exploded

near a schoolhouse in Istanbul
Fourteen Turkish children were killed

> TREVOR *closes her mouth. She opens it. War sounds.*

TV ANNOUNCER *(cont.)*
Then two ethnic groups
clashed outside a church in Nairobi
Twelve Kenyans were killed

> TREVOR *closes her mouth.*

MELANIE
Why won't you say something?

TREVOR
I just did

MELANIE
Something real

> *A beat.*

> TREVOR *lays a pillow beneath* MELANIE's *head.*

> *She stares at* MELANIE *a moment.*

FBI MAN *(quietly)*
Collateral damage.

> *The* FBI MAN *moves toward her, unseen.*

> *They sense each other.*

> *They move around each other. The We Sense Each Other dance.*

FBI MAN *(cont.)*
Ho ho . . .
Look at you
The mistress stumbles into
the black widow's web . . .

> TREVOR *draws closer.*

FBI MAN *(cont.)* *(to TREVOR)*
You're welcome.
(A beat.)
   (To audience.)
   At that moment
   I got a disturbing phone call

         He gets a phone call. He answers it.

FBI MAN *(cont.)*
Yello.
   (. . .)
   Uh-huhm.
   (. . .)
   Uh-huhm.
   (. . .)
   Uh-huhm.
   (. . .)
   WHAT?
   (. . .)
   I'm on it.
(Closes his phone. To us. Utter disbelief, betrayal.)
She bought two plane tickets to a foreign land
   Leaving 9:00 PM tonight

         TREVOR disappears.

FBI MAN *(cont.)* *(miffed, pacing)*
She's leaving?
   With whom?
   And why?
   When she's *this* close?
   It doesn't make sense.

What am I missing?
   What am I missing?
   What am I fucking fucking missing?

The FBI MAN *dons autumnal camouflage. He sneaks over to the house and peers into the window. He sees* WILLIAM *poring over papers.*

He removes some sort of listening device from his person and presses it against the window pane.

WILLIAM	FBI MAN
Focus	Focus
Focus	Focus
Focus	Focus

Moments of listening.

Then: TREVOR *enters.*

The FBI MAN *perks up and leans in.*

· *I Can't Find My Forks*

WILLIAM *(not looking up)*
Oh hey, Killer

TREVOR
Sorry to interrupt—

WILLIAM
No, no
    Just stuck on this one chapter
    "The Coadunation of Barbarity and Elegance
    in the Work of Trevor Pratt"
    I feel like I can't actually unpack it
    Until I know more about your / current piece

TREVOR
William—

WILLIAM
I know, I know
   I'm not asking you to talk about it
   I'm just telling you why I'm stuck.

TREVOR
It's finished.

     A small beat.

WILLIAM
Finished-finished?

TREVOR
Yeah.

WILLIAM
Really?
   Oh my God
   When can I see it?
   Or should I wait for the opening?
   That might be better
   Or I could interview you now
   and then take a peek later
   Totally up to you
   Though to be honest
   I'm dying to see it
   No pressure
   None whatsoever

     TREVOR *retrieves a suitcase and hands it to* WILLIAM.

WILLIAM *(cont.)*
What's this?

TREVOR
Shoes, shorts, socks, shirts, slacks
   Not your favorite corduroys

You won't need them
  Also they're disgusting and full of holes

WILLIAM
Is this for press?
  Or a quick vacay before the stampede?

TREVOR
I rolled your iPod in your green shirt
  You may want to take it out for the plane ride

WILLIAM (*delighted*)
Plane ride?
  Fancy!

TREVOR
Gum, batteries
  That book on sadism and aesthetics
  Lip balm
  Sunscreen

  I packed one for Randy too

WILLIAM
Randy's coming?
  Well gosh you're certainly thorough
  Where's your bag?

TREVOR
I'm not going

>   TREVOR *hands* WILLIAM *two plane tickets.*

WILLIAM (*reading tickets*)
Puerto Rico?
  These are / open-ended tickets

TREVOR
Your plane leaves tonight at nine

RANDY *storms in, panicked.*

RANDY
I can't find my forks

TREVOR
They're in your suitcase

RANDY
Why are they in my suitcase?
    Why were you in my room?

TREVOR
You're going on an adventure

RANDY
For how long?

TREVOR
Hard to say

RANDY
Will I miss your opening?

TREVOR
Yes, / Randy

RANDY
This is BULLSHIT
    This is BULLSHIT
    She wants the spotlight all for herself

WILLIAM
Take a chill, pal
    Nothing is in stone
    We can all talk about this like rational / people

RANDY
I don't want an adventure!
    I want to be on TV!

TREVOR
Randy—

RANDY
YOU HORRIBLE FREAKY BITCH.
  I HATE YOU BOTH!!!!
  FUCK YOU!!!!!!!!!!!

WILLIAM
Randy!

> RANDY *does a weird aggressive dance move and exits.*
>
> *A beat.*

WILLIAM *(cont.)*
Good lord.
  He's so sensitive.

TREVOR
That's a word—

WILLIAM
Muffin.
  Look at me.
  Is this about Melanie?

TREVOR
No—

WILLIAM
Had I known she'd be so *adhesive* / I would have never

TREVOR
This isn't about Melanie!
  I don't want you here for my opening.

WILLIAM
Randy can handle it
  His new therapist / seems to be wor—

TREVOR
It's YOU, William.

> *A small beat.*

WILLIAM
Trev
When I let you use those photos of Diane
I took my hands off the wheel.
I signed up for this.
All of it.

TREVOR *(suddenly vicious)*
Okay, look.
I'm, I'm sick.
Sick of your intellectual postscripts
your fame whoredom
your cloying regard
And I'm so fucking sick
of being the one thing
that makes your career feel important.

> *A beat.*

> WILLIAM *packs up his papers.*

WILLIAM
If this is how you need to be supported, fine.

But you didn't need to say any of that.

> WILLIAM *exits with his suitcase.* TREVOR *is stricken. She has some sort of strange gasping breakdown. But she recovers. She sings the keeper of the marvel song to calm herself.*

> *The* FBI MAN *is beaming, glowing.*

FBI MAN *(warm, impressed)*
The captain going down with her ship.
That's my girl.

TREVOR *freezes.*

FBI MAN *(cont.)* (*like a little kid.*)
God, I have so many questions!
   Are you claustrophobic?
   Are you a meticulous self-groomer?
   Do you enjoy scalding hot showers?
   Do you get impatient with slow drivers?
   Do you abide by the following tenets:
   strictness, diligence, decisiveness?
   Do you think cruelty is the only true universal language?

   And more and more and more!
   Gaps to fill, dots to connect . . .

   And maybe you'll want to know about me too?

   "Who is this bloodhound who's been tracking me?
   Where does he go at night?
   How many languages does he know?"
   (Seven.)
   "What is his moral imperative?"
   (To serve my country.)
   "What does he look like naked?"
   (A stallion.)
   (*He giggles. But then. He frowns.*)
   What am I saying?
   Snap out of it, man
   You're a professional
   Claim yourself
   Who are you?
   Who are you?

      He does some martial arts.

You are
the last of a dying breed

Get the job done
Get it done, asshole.
Make her fear you.
Make her fear herself.
Make her sizzle in the white beam of your righteousness.
And admit defeat.
(*Refreshed.*)
Ladies and gents
The time is nigh

The interview to end all interviews

Spotlight on TREVOR.

FBI MAN *(cont.)*
Trevor Pratt
   Thirty
   Primary subject of observation
   Achieved a cultish following for a photo series
   Poor eating habits
   No siblings
   Mother was a journalist
   Father was a hair model
   Has tiny hands and an avid mouth
   (*Does an incredible, eerie impression of* TREVOR.)
   "I said 'don't touch the art'

   My hands were like this the whole time
   Tell me you can handle it
   Buy a bright red belt
   This is going to hurt like a motherfucker

   You'll be rewarded
   When the doors are flung open"

        The FBI MAN *changes into a bumbling reporter outfit.*

TREVOR *appears on the screen. She is nervous. She is putting on makeup and fixing her hair.*

FBI MAN *(cont.)*
Dolling herself up
 Like a little painted peanut

> *The* FBI MAN *is uncharacteristically nervous.*

> *He wipes his hands on his slacks.*

FBI MAN *(cont.)*
Sweaty. Jeez. Okay.
(*He emboldens himself.*)
Focus. And.

> *He enters.*

• *A Straw Might Help*

> TREVOR's *studio. A new piece is in the center of the room, covered in a tarp.*

> *A knock.*

TREVOR
It's unlocked.

> FBI MAN *enters.* TREVOR *is busy fussing around the room, preparing, and does not fully register him at first.*

TREVOR
Welcome
Would you like some coffee?
It's strong
So strong your ends will split

FBI MAN
That will be fine.

>   *She scurries off to get coffee.*

TREVOR
Thanks for coming all the way up here
I know it's a long drive
Making *The New York Times* come to me, what a shitbag I am . . .
The photographers are on their way too
I just got a text

>   *She brings him a cup and takes a long drink of coffee herself.*
>   *Most of it dribbles down her chin.*

FBI MAN
Um . . .

TREVOR
Excuse me
I usually drink it iced.

FBI MAN
That happens a lot?

TREVOR
I can't feel my face anymore

FBI MAN
Oh.
A straw might help

TREVOR
Good idea.

>   *Then, it dawns on her.*

You're not my *Times* reporter . . .

>   *He smiles. She gasps.*

TREVOR *(cont.)*
It's you.
The exterminator.

> *Thunderclap, or the dramatic equivalent.*

FBI MAN
It is I.

TREVOR
Okay
I've been waiting for this—

FBI MAN
Not so fast.
I have a few questions

TREVOR
Of course you do

> *He circles her like an animal. He wants to enjoy this moment.*
> *Take his time. Relish her fear.*

FBI MAN
Trevor Pratt
Famous artist
Loved by many
Feared by none

Is that your goal?
To make people fear you?

TREVOR
No

FBI MAN
Then?

TREVOR
I want to make the reality of my culture
    conscious of itself

By confronting the transgressive nature
of modern spectatorship
in regards to human anguish

FBI MAN
That's a mouthful.

TREVOR
Are you being deferential or condescending?

FBI MAN
Does it matter?

TREVOR
Only if you care what I think of you.

FBI MAN
I do if it affects what you tell me.

TREVOR
Then I choose neither.

FBI MAN
Ho ho . . .
Too bad *I'm* the one calling the shots here

> *He moves in quick, like a fox.*

Here's a fun question.
Why do you want people to die?

TREVOR
I don't
I want them to feel the *potential*

FBI MAN
But these animals are lethal

TREVOR
How do you know?
They weren't tested

FBI MAN
Don't be coy
You've been injecting them—

TREVOR
With painkillers
That's not illegal

FBI MAN
You lie!
A human being has perished from contact!
Maybe more!

TREVOR
The animals *may* be infected
But they may not
I wouldn't know
I found them on the side of the road

> *A beat.* FBI MAN *turns to the audience.*

FBI MAN
Pause a moment here.

So crafty!
And much skinnier in person
her fingers are longer too
The curve of her back—

TREVOR
Un-pause

FBI MAN
Agk—
How did—
(*Nevermind. Now he means business.*)
Alright, Angelface
Let's have a dose of straight talk.

1) You have compromised the health and security of our nation
2) You have committed acts of biological warfare
3) You are a terrorist
4) You will be in prison for a very long time

TREVOR
You don't have anything on me

FBI MAN
I don't *need* anything
I have ways of making people talk

> *He tries his eye trick on* TREVOR. *But somehow it doesn't work. She advances on him.*

TREVOR
What makes you think you deserve to be here
Seeing what I've built
Feeling things I let you feel
Becoming part of my story

> *He tries it again. No go.*

FBI MAN (*to the audience, panicking re: his eye trick*)
It isn't working

> *To her.*

Just who do you think you are?

> *Trevor smiles.*

TREVOR
I am the keeper of the marvel.

> *Somehow she reverses the eye's effect. The* FBI MAN *begins to wither. The room changes.*

FBI MAN
I had a vegetable garden when I was twelve
 It was infested with grubs

I'd brush them gently off the leaves
Then collect them in tinfoil
and let them loose outside
Six years later I joined the army
Got sent to the Gulf
Nine years after that
I was rollerblading in my neighborhood
I rolled over a caterpillar
Saw its guts explode from one of its sides

TREVOR
You saw its guts
    You were riding pretty slowly

FBI MAN
It was on purpose.

TREVOR
Do you ever want to punish others
    for things you find horrible in yourself?

FBI MAN
Every day.

TREVOR
I know why you lost that eye

FBI MAN
Why?

TREVOR
Because you're a patriot.

       She strokes his scar throughout the following.

TREVOR *(cont.)* *(quietly)*
They used the prongs of a dirty dinner fork
After eating a meal of roasted lamb

You were so hungry

You remember the smell of the meal
More than the pain

The one who did it
Was the kindest of the three
He moved quickly
And avoided the lid
So you could close it afterwards

They threatened to cook it and feed it to you
But they didn't want you to gain strength from the eating
So they fed it to their dogs
While you watched with your other eye

When you were rescued by your men
They gave you the privilege of avenging yourself
Which you did
One by one
In private

And
You took your fucking time

>   *A beat. The room changes back. FBI MAN is a little lost.*

Now I want you to tell me something else.

FBI MAN
Okay

TREVOR
I want you to say it quietly

FBI MAN
Okay

TREVOR
And I don't want you to look at me as you say it

FBI MAN
Okay

> *Beat.*

> TREVOR *pulls the tarp from the final piece of art.* MELANIE
> *is strapped to the metal, dying.*

TREVOR
How?

FBI MAN
I—
   I told her to touch them

TREVOR
Why?

FBI MAN
For you.

> *A beat.*

TREVOR
There are about fifty photographers outside that door
   It's not too late to disappear

> *A small beat.*

FBI MAN
My loyalty to my vocation
My years of alienation and solitude
Suddenly
They're here
Two feet behind me

   And you
You're eleven inches in front of me

I've been living my life for this very moment.

> *A beat. The* FBI MAN *does not help* MELANIE.

TREVOR
So have I.

> TREVOR *flings open the door of the shed. The paparazzi begins snapping shots of the scene. Flashbulbs pop maniacally.*

> TREVOR *smiles for the cameras and holds her arms out.*

> *After a beat, the* FBI MAN *also smiles for the cameras.*

• *Coda: A-Waitin'*

> *Eventually,* TREVOR *and the* FBI MAN *disappear.*

> *Lights change.* MELANIE *and the* ANIMALS *sing this final song.*

MELANIE and the ANIMALS
I dream of a villa on an Italian coast
  wrought iron
  white muslin
  flowers
  a tree

  An outdoor dinner table with chairs for two
  white marble
  wine glasses
  linens
  and me

  I dream the chairs are overturned
  The glasses not filled

The wine not chilled
And there I sit
In my summer gown
a-waitin'
a-waitin'
a-waitin' . . .

A-waitin' . . . for you . . .

      Blackout.

THAT PRETTY PRETTY; OR, THE RAPE PLAY

PRODUCTION HISTORY

That Pretty Pretty; Or, the Rape Play had its world premiere on February 10, 2009, at Rattlestick Playwrights Theatre. Director: Kip Fagan. Set design: Narelle Sissons. Costume design: Jessica Pabst. Lighting design: Matthew Frey. Sound design: Eric Shim. Prop design: Mary Robinette Kowal. Fight choreography: Rick Sordelet. Technical director: Brian Smallwood. Production stage manager: Katrina Renee Herrmann.

AGNES	Lisa Joyce
VALERIE	Danielle Slavick
RODNEY	Joseph Gomez
OWEN	Greg Keller
JANE FONDA/JANE	Annie McNamara

CHARACTERS

AGNES   female, trashy, sexy, disarmingly
                   angelic

VALERIE   female, bullish, tough, crazy sexy

RODNEY   male, fit, charismatic, chill and yet
                   oddly dangerous

OWEN   male, sensitive hipster-ish dude

JANE FONDA/JANE   female, circa '82, leg warmers et al.

SETTING

Anytown, America.

TIME

Now.

NOTES

A stroke (/) marks the point of interruption in overlapping dialogue. When the stroke is not immediately followed by text, the next line should occur on the last syllable of the word before the slash—not an overlap but a concise interruption.

ACKNOWLEDGMENT

The section of the play where the women throw themselves onto the ground in choreographed fits is an edited excerpt from Charles L. Mee's play *Big Love*.

PROLOGUE

VALERIE and AGNES appear in the darkness, face-forward, in single lights. Bon Jovi's "You Give Love a Bad Name" is playing faintly in the background. A fellow croons along dismally and drunkenly with the song.

AGNES
Val?

VALERIE
Yeah?

AGNES
I'm a little drunk.

VALERIE
You drink too much.

AGNES
What state are we in?

VALERIE
You're a dumbass.

AGNES
We've done this a lot.

VALERIE
I know.

AGNES
We're gonna run out of states.

VALERIE

Dumbass SUPREME. We still have Colorado, Delaware, Michigan, Louisiana, Alabama, Arkansas, / Ohio, Missouri, Nebraska, North Carolina

AGNES

Then we'll get caught. Or something. I don't want . . . um . . .

VALERIE

I thought we didn't care if we got caught.

AGNES

We just . . . wanna keep going for as long as we can. Because we fucking HATE THEM ALL. Okay. Not just the ones with bombs in their trunks.

VALERIE

That's right.

AGNES

And we hate fucking people telling us how to act.

VALERIE

Right.

AGNES

About our bodies.

VALERIE

Right.

AGNES

And the Internet.

VALERIE

Sure.

AGNES

And the radio. I'm hungry.

VALERIE
You're always hungry.

AGNES
The food sucks here. And there's none left.

VALERIE
You have a problem.

AGNES
If there was more food I wouldn't be drunk because I would of eaten enough and the food would be absorbing the vodka. When you wanna go over?

VALERIE
When he finishes his karaoke song.

AGNES
Right on. (*A beat, tone change.*) Sometimes I think you love me too much.

> *A long beat.*

VALERIE
Delete delete delete delete delete delete delete.

> *End of Prologue.*

> *Lights up.*

> VALERIE *and* AGNES *stumble into a posh hotel room in fur coats.* AGNES *is wearing a bonnet and* VALERIE *a straw hat. Beneath their coats their outfits are outrageously skimpy.*

> *Something feels very fake about the whole setup . . . perhaps the set is too vivid, perhaps everyone is a little too enthusiastic.*

> *The acting in the following seen should be completely and artificially over-the-top intense. Lots of volume.*

AGNES
Where is he you fucking lost him / already.

VALERIE
He was right behind you don't freak on me.

AGNES
He's mine Val.

VALERIE
Where's the minibar . . . ROCK!

>   VALERIE *goes to the minibar.*

AGNES
HE'S MINE / VALERIE.

VALERIE
Shhhh.

>   AGNES *tosses herself on the bed and begins bouncing.*
>   VALERIE *cannot open the minibar.*

AGNES
I'm the ho here. Just remember that. This bed smells like starch and marinated ass . . . I like hotels I like hotels I like hotels.

VALERIE
Locked? Fuck . . .

>   RODNEY *stumbles in behind them. He is red-faced and*
>   *wears a tie and a sombrero.*

RODNEY
Wasted!

AGNES
Wasted!

>   RODNEY *falls on the bed on top of* AGNES.

RODNEY

This place is decent . . .

AGNES

My uncle works for the chain.

>   *They begin to kiss.*

VALERIE

Hey. HEY. Hey Agnes. Show him your new dance, you slutty whore.

AGNES

I made up a dance.

RODNEY

Go on.

VALERIE

Slutty little whore.

AGNES

I don't have a name yet for it.

RODNEY

Do they have whiskey?

VALERIE

I can't get the fucker open . . .

>   VALERIE *kicks at the minibar furiously. It swings open. She*
>   *begins rooting around inside.*

AGNES

You aren't watching . . .

VALERIE

Go.

>   AGNES *does a complicated hip-hop move.* RODNEY
>   *applauds.*

VALERIE *(cont.)*
She made it for Howard Stern.

AGNES
Shut UP.

VALERIE
She thinks if she can get on the air, he'll ask her to dance.

AGNES
Most people think he's gross but he's got these ice-blue eyes, that's why he wears sunglasses all the time.

> VALERIE *pulls out a digital camera and begins shooting pictures of the room.*

AGNES *(cont.)*
You're like psycho with that shit.

VALERIE
For the blog . . .

> VALERIE *aims the camera at* AGNES. AGNES *giggles and begins to strip.*

RODNEY
You girls aren't really sisters, are you . . .

AGNES
We came out of the same womb . . .

RODNEY
You're wild. You are wild.

VALERIE
Are you two ready to kick it or will I stand here like a douchebag?

> AGNES *begins to take off her bonnet.*

RODNEY
Leave the bonnet on.

AGNES *and* RODNEY *begin to maul each other.* VALERIE
lights a cigarette and watches.

AGNES
She's letting me have you first, she NEVER does that.

RODNEY *(to VALERIE)*
Come here . . .

VALERIE
I'm fine.

RODNEY
I paid for both . . .

AGNES
Come on Val . . .

VALERIE
I'm thirsty . . . I'm going outside for a / Diet Coke

RODNEY
Do not leave the fucking room.

> *A beat.* VALERIE *reaches into her purse and pulls out a gun.*

RODNEY *(cont.)*
Wait.

> VALERIE *shoots* RODNEY *in the head. Blood hits the wall
> and the floor.*

AGNES
GROSS. Gross gross gross get him off me . . .

> VALERIE *helps get* RODNEY *off* AGNES. *They roll him
> onto the floor.*

AGNES *(cont.)*
You're kind of harsh sometimes. Get one for the blog.

> VALERIE *shoots a picture of the dead* RODNEY.

AGNES *(cont.)*
Should I get in it too?

VALERIE
Yeah . . . pose a little.

      AGNES *starts to remove the bonnet.*

VALERIE *(cont.)*
Keep the fucking bonnet on.

      VALERIE *begins snapping photos of* AGNES *in various poses with the dead* RODNEY.

AGNES
I hate fat people. There were SO MANY fat people tonight. The women all wore dainty little boots with little toothpick heels and they had fucking ENORMOUS cankles . . . And the FUCKING HATS!! What's the point of a hat party, even?

VALERIE
It wasn't a hat party, dumbass. It was a benefit.

AGNES
I've been to benefits where they didn't bring out a barrel of hats. Who the fuck gave those right-wing fucks the idea they'd have more fun with hats on their fat fucking heads? Hey. Jesus had a beard, right?

VALERIE
Yeah.

AGNES
I pictured him clean-shaven for a second. I wish we had gotten there before all the food got eaten . . . I want new breasts, do you think we can buy me some?

VALERIE
You don't need them anymore.

AGNES
I may have quit stripping but I still like my body to look slammin'. . .

VALERIE
Make him talk.

AGNES *grabs hold of* RODNEY'*s bottom lip.*
AGNES
"Fetus fetus fetus fetus holy fucking shit I love that fetus and Jesus loves the fetus too, and just remember it ain't where life begins but where LOVE begins . . ." (*A beat.*) You could have let me fuck him first, Val. I was getting wet and everything . . .

VALERIE
He's a lousy lay . . .

AGNES
You can't tell by just looking at him.

VALERIE
He's got a cashew dick. Look.

AGNES *checks it out.*

AGNES
How did you know?

VALERIE
I did him in the bathroom while you were on the buffet table.

AGNES
You wouldn't.

VALERIE
Who asked you to get up on the goddamn buffet table, Agnes? Who asked you to do that?

AGNES
I had something to say.

VALERIE

You make an ass of yourself when you stand on a buffet table. You make like you have no self-respect. That is tedious and it's UGLY.

AGNES

Just because I don't have a blog doesn't mean I don't have something to say.

VALERIE

And no one heard you over the Quiet Riot. And you could have slipped and fallen, like that time on your garage door.

> *They stare at each other a moment. Something subtle changes in* VALERIE.

> *She opens her computer and begins to type furiously.* AGNES *does not hear her speak.*

VALERIE *(cont.)*

Words words words. Come on, sucka. This gal is a real beeyotch. BITCH SUPREME. Talkin' shit about her manifesto . . . ridding the world of shitbags trying to jam their laws into her uterus . . . Lots of fucks. Fuck fuck fuck. What else . . . OH! She's a secret dyke! HA, YES!!! Wants to get her freak on with Agnes! But wait, they're sisters. Think on this, come back to it later. Maybe she should be more angry, or like. Oh, and super hot. A super hot angry dyke. She's a HATER. RAAAR! YEAH!! LIKE AN ANIMAL!!!

> VALERIE *springs up from her chair.*

AGNES

Where are you going?

VALERIE

DIET COKE!

AGNES

From where?

VALERIE
VENDING MACHINE!

AGNES
Get me a seltzer please.

VALERIE
IF THEY DON'T HAVE?

AGNES
Diet Coke.

> VALERIE *leaves.* AGNES *manipulates* RODNEY's *mouth again.*

AGNES *(cont.)*
"She smelled like grilled cheese and mustard." Man I'm hungry. Wonder if they do room service here. But wait! I don't eat. I am a crazy skinny obsessed monster. AND, I spend my days and nights plotting on how to be a skinnier version of myself . . . Also, I have a lot of sex with men who aren't my boyfriend. Sometimes my boyfriend loves me too much, and that makes me go apeshit with other guys. Maybe I'm afraid of commitment. Maybe that's why I hate on these dudes. At any rate, I have no self-respect. Awesome.

> AGNES *straddles* RODNEY's *leg and begins humping it.*

> VALERIE *returns with two Diet Cokes.*

AGNES *(cont.)*
Val . . . do the other leg . . .

VALERIE
Uh-uh.

AGNES
Come on . . .

VALERIE
I'm drinking my Diet Coke.

VALERIE *connects her camera to the computer.* AGNES *grabs* RODNEY'*s bottom lip again as she humps.*

AGNES
"I like really skinny girls. How'd you get so fucking skinny . . ." Starving myself and drinking water and longboarding my face off . . . I can't wait 'til summer . . . my metabolism speeds up in the summer . . . I'd burn more calories during sex if it took me longer to get off . . .

VALERIE
Then take longer . . .

AGNES
I . . . can't . . .

AGNES *climaxes.* VALERIE *hands* AGNES *a Diet Coke.*

VALERIE
The ice machine was broken. Hundred-fifty a room, you'd think you could . . . wait a second. (*Tone change.*) RAR! HUNDRED-FIFTY A ROOM, YOU'D THINK YOU COULD GET SOME FUCKING ICE!

AGNES
Complain to the management.

VALERIE *picks up the phone and dials zero.*

VALERIE
HI . . . YEAH, THE ICE MACHINE ISN'T WORKING, COCKWEED! . . . NO, JUST HALF A BUCKET IS FINE . . . THANKS, COCKWEED. (*She hangs up.*) HE'LL BE RIGHT UP!

AGNES
You didn't call / him

VALERIE (*re: her computer*)
ROCKNESS!! THEY HAVE WI-FI! (*Typing.*) Rockness, bitches . . . I'm the Rockness Monster . . .

AGNES *(bored)*
I should piss the bed. Dare me?

> AGNES *jumps on the bed and drops her pants.*

AGNES
Dare me, quick! 'Cause even if you don't I'll still do it . . .

VALERIE
I dare you.

AGNES *(tries to pee)*
Pee, pee . . . Ssssss . . . argh, performance anxiety!!! Wait . . .
there's a trickle . . .

> AGNES *pees in the bed.*

AGNES *(cont.)*
I'M PEEING IN THE BED! I'M PEEING IN THE BED! HOW
FUCKING AWESOME IS THAT?

VALERIE
Completely.

> *A beat.* AGNES *is bored again.*

AGNES
You think there's a piano here?

VALERIE
No.

AGNES
I love to play the piano. I dream of dinner parties and fancy linens, I dream of myself playing piano beautifully afterwards, like a
recital, with everyone applauding. So classy.

> *A beat. Subtle change.*

AGNES	VALERIE
Shit. I'm not at all classy. I'm a skanky ho.	Shit. You're not at all classy. You're a skanky ho.
I secretly think it would make me like elegant if I could play like, really really well.	You secretly think it would make you like, elegant if you could play like, really really well.
That's deep. And messed up. How the fuck am I gonna pull that off?	How the fuck am I gonna pull that off?
More on this later.	

In the following, underlined words are spoken by both women.

AGNES *(cont.)*
Do they get Howard Stern in Mississippi?

VALERIE
I AM SO FUCKING SICK OF HEARING ABOUT HOWARD FUCKING STERN!! Too angry? Too angry?

AGNES
Oh damn. He's on Sirius. I need satellite to get him. Do I have satellite?

VALERIE
You are dumber than a bag of dumb, Agnes. You should have the word DUMBASS tattooed across your forehead so when dudes fuck you they won't think they're fucking the smart out of you. *(Tone change.)* That's really harsh. Agnes isn't retarded, or. She's just like, manipulative. I'm losing it.

AGNES
I'm not retarded. I'm just manipulative. My dumbness is like, a cover. I'm conflicted, therefore I hide behind stupidity. Ooh, folksy. Work that. Hey Valerie. When you were fucking my husband, did he talk about God at all?

VALERIE
Which time?

AGNES
The last time.

> VALERIE *says nothing a moment.* AGNES *grabs her own bottom lip.*

AGNES *(cont.)*
"No Agnes. He was talking about you."

VALERIE
No Agnes. He was talking about you.

AGNES *(lets go of her lip)*
Okay.

VALERIE
Okay. Wait. No. Who was fucking whose / husband?

AGNES
Who was fucking whose <u>husband</u>?

VALERIE
I'm <u>losing it</u>. I gotta change it <u>up</u>. <u>Okay</u>, let's get SUBTEXTY. The STAKES HAVE BEEN RAISED!

> AGNES *and* VALERIE *become a bad Pinter play.*

AGNES
What did you think of the DJ?

> *A beat.*

VALERIE
He was all right.

> *A beat.*

AGNES
I love '80s rock.

A beat.

VALERIE
Do you?

> *As an answer,* **AGNES** *jumps up on top of the bed and begins singing "Still of the Night" by Whitesnake and miming David Coverdale from the video. This is an act of aggression, but it is super sexy.*

AGNES
In the still of the night I hear the wolf howl, honey
Sniffin' around yer daw
In the still of the night
I feel my heart feelin' heavay
Tellin' me I godda have mo-wore

> *She mimes a guitar.* **VALERIE** *watches her.*

AGNES
Remember in the video, the guitar solo, it gets all smoky he's like shadowy and silhouettey and on his knees, and he whips out a fucking BOW, like for a violin, and starts BOWING his guitar on his knees and practically humping the guitar . . . I would get off to that like twice an hour.

VALERIE
You are so pretty. (*A beat.*) FUCK! Damn it, Agnes! You see what you do? "Wah, you're so pretty, wah . . ." Like a cancer. Bulldog, where's the bulldog? KEEP THE FUCKING BULLDOG!

> **VALERIE** *barks like a rabid dog.*

AGNES
Is it working?

VALERIE
I don't know.

AGNES
Can I do something?

VALERIE
Hit me in the face. Get me angry, get me all riled up.

AGNES
Fist or palm?

VALERIE
Fist. No, palm.

> AGNES *hits* VALERIE *in the face.*

VALERIE *(cont.)*
Again.

> AGNES *hits* VALERIE *in the face.*

VALERIE *(cont.)*
Try to get your ring into it.

> AGNES *turns her ring around on her finger and smacks*
> VALERIE *again.*

VALERIE *(cont.)*
Am I bleeding?

AGNES
No.

VALERIE
One more.

> AGNES *hits* VALERIE *in the face.*

VALERIE
Okay.

AGNES
You mad?

VALERIE
Yeah.

AGNES
Furious?

VALERIE
Yeah, yeah. Thanks.

> AGNES *hits* VALERIE *in the face again.*

VALERIE *(cont.)*
Enough!

AGNES
Hit me back!

VALERIE
Later . . . I need to ride this out . . .

> AGNES *sulks on the bed.* VALERIE *is about to type.*

VALERIE *(cont.)*
Kick it, homes . . . smack that juicy groove . . . (*She types nothing. A beat. Forlorn.*) I'm lost.

> *An uber-chipper* JANE FONDA *enters, dressed in leg warmers and a headband. She begins doing aerobics for us.*

VALERIE *(cont.)*
Jane Fonda . . . thank God.

JANE FONDA
My workout is designed to build strength, develop flexibility, and increase endurance. To get the full benefit from the workout you must do it with me from beginning to end without stopping. It is this vigorous and sustained use of your entire body that will not only tone your muscles but will burn up calories, improve your circulation, eliminate toxins, and strengthen your heart and lungs. The basis of the workout is the repetition of certain movements that use a single muscle group against the resistance of your own body weight.

(*A beat.*) You see how excellent I am? An inspiration. Generations of women look up to me. Do I inspire fear in you? I shouldn't. Glow glow glow, sparkle like a star. I am not someone who dominates. I am frank and dignified. I am sincere. I have loads of confidence, except when I feel abused, and then I simply raise my chin and take it. THAT'S a real woman. THAT'S heroic. And I have a kickin' bod.

> JANE FONDA *begins doing an aerobics routine to the following song, which is "Pretty Baby" by Kay Starr.*

JANE FONDA **(cont.)** *(singing)*
Everybody loves a baby
  That's why I'm in love with you,
  Pretty Baby, Pretty Baby
  And I'd like to be your sister, brother,
  Dad and mother too,
  Pretty Baby, Pretty Baby.

  Won't you come and let me rock you
  In my cradle of love,
  We'll cuddle all the time.
  Oh, I want a Lovin' Baby
  And it might as well be you,
  Pretty Baby of mine!

> *She does an aerobics-y soft-shoe.* VALERIE *and* AGNES *join her on the soft-shoe, then they all sing together.*

JANE FONDA, AGNES, and VALERIE *(singing)*
Everybody loves a baby
  That's why I'm in love with you,
  Pretty Baby, (*whistle*) Pretty Baby;
  And I'd like to be your family
  Aunts and uncles, cousins too
  Pretty Baby, Pretty Baby.

  Won't you come and let me rock you
  In my cradle of love,

We'll cuddle all a'the time.
I want a baby and I'm countin' on you
You're my honey
You are my Daddy
That's why it's gotta be you!

> *They finish the song and aerobicize themselves offstage.*

> *The stage is bare for quite a while.*

> JANE FONDA *escorts* RODNEY *and* OWEN *in, as though they were two dapper paramours. They are young, scruffy, your typical thirty-something slackers. One is wearing a bonnet and the other a straw hat.*

OWEN
Thank you, Jane.

RODNEY
Thank you, Jane.

> *They tip their hats to* JANE FONDA.

> JANE FONDA *nods and exits. Lights change.*

> *This scene is identical in tone to the previous hotel scene: fake, vivid, incredibly loud.*

RODNEY *(cont.)*
Where is she you fucking lost her / already.

OWEN
She was right behind you don't freak on me.

RODNEY
She's mine Owen.

OWEN
Where's the minibar . . . rock.

> OWEN *goes to the minibar.*

RODNEY
SHE'S MINE / OWEN.

OWEN
Shhhh.

>   RODNEY *tosses himself on the bed and begins bouncing.*

RODNEY
This bed smells like starch and marinated ass . . . I like hotels I
like hotels I like hotels.

OWEN
Okay, this is better. Feeling it now, feeling it. I'm here, The Rod
is here, we are IN THE MOTHERFUCKIN' HIZZY. Now let's
DO THIS THING.

>   OWEN *cannot open the minibar.*

OWEN
Locked? Jesus . . .

>   AGNES *stumbles in behind them. She is red-faced and wears a*
>   *gown and a sombrero.*

AGNES
Wasted!

RODNEY
Wasted!

>   AGNES *falls on the bed on top of* RODNEY.

AGNES
This place is decent . . .

RODNEY
My uncle works for the chain.

>   *They begin to kiss.*

OWEN

Whoa. That feels really shitty, watching them do that. (*To* ROD-NEY.) Hey. HEY. Hey RODNEY. Show her your new dance.

RODNEY

I made up a dance.

AGNES

Go on.

RODNEY

I don't have a name yet for it.

AGNES

Do they have whiskey?

OWEN

I can't get it open . . .

> OWEN *kicks at the minibar furiously. It swings open. He begins rooting around inside.*

RODNEY

You aren't watching . . .

OWEN

Go.

> RODNEY *does a complicated hip-hop move.* AGNES *applauds.*

OWEN *(cont.)*

He made it for Howard Stern.

RODNEY

Shut UP, dude.

> RODNEY *grabs* AGNES *by the hair. She does not react.*

OWEN

He thinks if he can get on the air, he'll ask him to dance.

RODNEY

Most people think he's gross but he's got these ice-blue eyes, that's why he wears sunglasses all the time.

> RODNEY *shoves* AGNES *onto the bed and presses his knee into her back, still holding her hair, and begins to tear off her clothes.*
>
> *Again, she does not react. As a matter of fact, it seems to have a calming, pleasant effect on her.*
>
> OWEN *pulls out a pack of cigarettes. He begins lighting them one by one and putting them out on* AGNES's *body.*

RODNEY *(cont.)*

You're like psycho with that shit.

OWEN

For the blog . . .

AGNES

You guys aren't really brothers, are you . . .

RODNEY

We came out of the same womb . . .

AGNES

You're wild. You are wild.

OWEN

Are you two ready to kick it or will I stand here like a douchebag?

> RODNEY *begins to take off his bonnet.*

AGNES

Leave the bonnet on.

> RODNEY *begins to tie* AGNES *up in the style of Abu Ghraib. He places a pillowcase over her head and attaches electric wires to her hands.*

RODNEY

He's letting me have you first, he NEVER does that.

> *He shocks her five times, and each time she lets out a shout of delight.*

OWEN

Sweet. That's some subversive shit right there. That is CONTRO-VERSIAL. But that's the point, right? When you hit a nerve? POLARIZING. Some people just don't have the stomach for social commentary. They want butterflies and Bambi. Well fuck 'em. Right? Not my audience. I'm not the man with the lullaby, my friends. I'm the man with the MACHETE. A fugitive. Slicing down your tidy little forests. Everything that makes you feel safe? Shing. The lies you tell yourself? Shing. Truth to power. Burn it down, bitches.

AGNES *(to OWEN)*

Come here . . .

OWEN

I'm fine.

AGNES

I paid for both . . .

RODNEY

Come on Owen . . .

OWEN

I'm thirsty . . . I'm going outside for a / Diet Coke.

AGNES

Do not leave the fucking room.

> *A beat.* **OWEN** *reaches into his coat and pulls out a gun.*

AGNES *(cont.)*

Wait.

OWEN *shoots* AGNES *in the face. Then he pulls a machete from his coat and hacks at her.*

OWEN
Shing! Taste the blade! Skeeee-rumptious!

Then he pulls a sledgehammer from the closet and begins slamming it into her. Blood hits the wall.

OWEN *(cont.)*
Rahg! World smells a whole lot better without your reeking hole . . .

He is finally done.

OWEN *(cont.)*
Sweet Jesus that felt good.

RODNEY
GROSS.

OWEN
But maybe a little much.

RODNEY
Gross gross gross get her off me . . .

OWEN *helps get* AGNES *off* RODNEY. *They roll her onto the floor.*

OWEN
I may cut the sledgehammer.

RODNEY
You're kind of harsh sometimes. Get one for the blog.

OWEN *poses with his cigarette in his mouth, one hand in a thumbs-up, and the other pointing to* AGNES's *genitals.*

RODNEY *(cont.)*
Should I get in it too?

OWEN
Yeah . . . pose a little.

      RODNEY *starts to remove the bonnet.*

OWEN *(cont.)*
Keep the fucking bonnet on.

      RODNEY *pretends to be raping* AGNES*'s body.*

OWEN *(cont.)*
Hoo-hoo! Beauteous.

RODNEY
I want a new dick, do you think we can buy me one?

OWEN
You don't need one anymore.

RODNEY
I may have quit raping but I still like my body to look slammin'. . .

OWEN
Make her talk.

      Lights change. AGNES *pops up. She looks gorgeous, all bloody and angelic in her gown.*

      OWEN *looks at her longingly.*

AGNES *(slowly, seductively)*
The table is set with gleaming silver, and everyone is wearing suits and gowns. I'm in one of those Academy Award jobbies, all long and shimmery. Everyone has just dined on pheasant and mints, and now they are sipping Turkish coffee. And then someone says, "Agnes, shall you play us a sonata?" And I say, "If you insist." And then I move toward the piano in my gown and place my long fingers on the keys, and I begin to play. And all the guests close their eyes and lean into one another. As though they have been dreaming of this moment.

OWEN *inhales deeply, intoxicated.*

OWEN *(with longing)*
I can smell your hair . . .

AGNES *drops back down again.*

OWEN **(cont.)** *(panic)*
Agnes . . .

Lights back to normal.

RODNEY
You could have let me fuck her first, Owen. I was getting hard and everything . . .

OWEN
She's a lousy lay . . .

RODNEY
You can't tell by just looking at her.

OWEN
She's selfish. Comes too fast. And loud. And she's a liar.

RODNEY
How do you know?

OWEN
Lies and bullshit, every word. "I love you, Owen." Bullshit. "I've loved you since the day you screamed at me about the garage door." Bullshit. Look at her. SLUT SUPREME. Had more cock than a poultry farm. She can't play the piano worth shit. She has no class. She won't shut the fuck up. She's a cancer. She takes over your mind. You wanna tear your eyeballs out and feed them to the cat!

JANE FONDA *enters and begins doing aerobics frantically.*

JANE FONDA
You're losing it, Owen . . .

OWEN
She takes over, Jane. She eats my mind. I can smell her.

JANE FONDA
It's still early . . . you have time . . .

OWEN
I'm lost.

> *Sudden darkness.*
>
> *A pause.*
>
> *All we hear are the two voices. We see nothing.*

AGNES *(V.O.)*
Owen? Are you crying?

OWEN *(V.O.)*
I have a cold.

AGNES *(V.O.)*
I wanna talk to you . . .

OWEN *(V.O.)*
I need to finish this, Agnes.

AGNES *(V.O.)*
Remember when we were kids and I rode my garage door to the top and let go and fell on the asphalt sideways and broke my leg, and you wouldn't stop screaming at me?

OWEN *(V.O.)*
Yeah . . .

AGNES *(V.O.)*
And remember last week I went from zero to psycho when that dude honked at me for pulling out too far and so I double flipped him off and made a retarded fuck-you face and you were shocked?

OWEN *(V.O.)*
Kind of . . .

AGNES *(V.O.)*
And remember when you stepped on my finger and I tried to fake-cry to make you feel bad but it didn't work?

OWEN *(V.O.)*
No.

AGNES *(V.O.)*
I was just thinking about all that, all at once. I don't know why. And when I think like that, my inner crazy comes out and I want to hit you for like, I don't know. Loving me too much.

OWEN *(V.O.)*
You shouldn't hit me, Agnes.

AGNES *(V.O.)*
I know.

OWEN *(V.O.)*
You should never hit me.

AGNES *(V.O.)*
Because it emasculates you.

OWEN *(V.O.)*
Because it is tedious and it's UGLY.

> *Sound of hitting.* AGNES *giggles. More hitting.*

OWEN *(cont.) (V.O.)*
Stop it.

AGNES *(V.O.)*
You love me.

OWEN *(V.O.)*
STOP. IT.

AGNES *(V.O.)*
You love me, Owen.

OWEN *(V.O.)*
I'm trying to work.

AGNES *(V.O.)*
You love me too much.

OWEN *(V.O.)*
Why do you have to say it like that?

> *Sound of a gun being cocked.*

OWEN *(cont.) (V.O.)*
Where the fuck did you get that?

AGNES *(V.O.)*
It's mine . . .

OWEN *(V.O.)*
Put it down, Agnes . . .

AGNES *(V.O.)*
I like holding it. Makes me feel like a badass.

OWEN *(V.O.)*
Put it DOWN . . .

AGNES *(V.O.)*
I like it when you're scared of me. I feel like I can do anything. (*A beat.*) You're not gonna cry, are you? Like a little bitch?

OWEN *(V.O.) (breaking)*
Agnes . . .

AGNES *(V.O.)*
Why don't you go put on a dress, faggot?

OWEN *(V.O.) (losing it)*
I can't do this. I can't / do this.

AGNES *(V.O.)*
YOU ARE A GAYWAD! A WAD OF GAY! Turd licker. Ass muncher.

OWEN *(V.O.)*
I CAN'T DO THIS!

AGNES *(V.O.)*
THEN TRY HARDER!

> *Lights change suddenly.*
>
> *We are in the dining hall of a very fancy room. A long table with a fine linen tablecloth is in the center of the room. The table is set for four, and on silver platters is a sumptuous spread of strange foods.*
>
> AGNES *is rolling on the floor in a gown.* OWEN *is wearing a suit and has a gunshot wound in his head. He and* VALERIE *are seated at the table waiting to eat. They are hungry, and anxious, but it appears they are waiting until the others get to the table before they start. They refuse to look at each other.*
>
> *Finally,* RODNEY *emerges in a suit and sits at the table and dabs his mouth with a napkin. He snaps his fingers and* AGNES *stops rolling. She seats herself at the table.*
>
> RODNEY *clasps his hands and the others follow suit. They all mumble the following at slightly different speeds:*

ALL
Bless us oh Lord and these thy gifts which we are about to receive from your bountiful hands through Christ our Lord amen.

> *They cross themselves and begin to eat. They eat politely, tensely, occasionally glancing at one another, passing the wine and grated cheese and bread. They eat for a very long tense time.*

VALERIE *can't take the tension any longer. She drops to the ground and begins rolling. After a moment* RODNEY, *irritated, snaps his fingers.* VALERIE *sullenly returns to her seat.*

They continue to eat, passing the gravy, the pepper, the peas.

After a long while, AGNES *speaks to* OWEN. *Tonally, this should resemble a British drawing room comedy—stiff and strange (sans accents).*

AGNES
Would someone please pass me a cashew?

VALERIE *giggles.* OWEN *puts food on* AGNES's *face.*

They continue to eat in silence for a long time.

RODNEY *(to VALERIE)*
I think there's something wrong with you.

VALERIE
What?

RODNEY
The way you eat.

VALERIE
Oh.

A long silence. VALERIE *tries to change the way she eats.*

JANE FONDA *appears and whips out a large pepper grinder.*

JANE FONDA
Black pepper?

RODNEY
Black pepper.

She grinds.

JANE FONDA
Black pepper?

OWEN
Black pepper.

> *She grinds.*

RODNEY
Thank you, Jane.

OWEN
Thank you, Jane.

> JANE FONDA, *frank and dignified, disappears.*

RODNEY
She's so frank and dignified.

OWEN
I know.

RODNEY
I wish all women were like her.

> *A long silence. People eating.*

> AGNES *is about to drink from the wine glass.*

OWEN (cont.)
You drink too much.

> AGNES *puts her wine glass back on the table without sipping.*

OWEN *(cont.)*
Don't fidget.

AGNES
I'm not.

OWEN
You're about to.

AGNES *does not fidget.*

Long silence. People eating and drinking.

VALERIE *reaches for the bread.* RODNEY *slaps her hand away.*

AGNES
Would anyone like me to play the piano?

OWEN
You can't fucking play the piano.

A long silence. People eating and drinking.

Suddenly, RODNEY *pushes back in his chair and begins to shout the following:*

RODNEY
Say. I have a funny story!

The others exclaim: "Really?" "Bravo!" "Fantastic, go on!"

RODNEY (cont.)
It's rather comical. I think you'll enjoy it. It's about the time I nearly lost all my money!

More exclamations: "My word!" "You don't say!"

RODNEY (cont.)
It's a completely true story. I really think you'll enjoy it. I was in the war!

More exclamations.

OWEN
Which war?

RODNEY
THE war. The one I was in! I was in the war. And we were in this country. And there were several of us. Old Eddie and old Ronnie and old Johnnie and old Billy and old Charlie and old Artie and

old Howie and old Rudy and old Jimmy and old Gary. And there was a cave. And the cave had two entrances. And we were chasing two guys. Two poop-flingers. We called them poop-flingers.

OWEN
Ha!

RODNEY
We called them poop-flingers because after they shat they wiped their asses with their hands and then flung their shit at the walls.

Exclamations: "No!" "They didn't!" "Disgusting!"

RODNEY *(cont.)*
And THEN they shook your hand.

More exclamations of disgust.

RODNEY *(cont.)* *(old war tale)*
So we were chasing these two poop-flingers across this prairie, weeellll it wasn't a *prairie* but it was a stretch of land not *unlike* a prairie except there were no prairie *dogs*, and then the land became rocks and the rocks turned into caves, and we were still chasing, and we weren't shooting because we knew about these caves and we knew the poop-flingers were running straight into the caves, and so we just chased them for a bunch of miles, and we lost sight of them because they were pretty fast, but then old Jimmy said he saw one of them disappear into the cave with two entrances, and so old Eddie and old Ronnie and old Johnnie and old Billy climbed over the rocks to the other side of the cave, and we waited for their signal, and when they were in position old Eddie screamed POOP TUBE!!! And they ran into the cave screaming, and the poop-flinger inside freaked and started running out the other side, and me and Charlie and Artie and Howie and Rudy and Jimmy and Gary were standing there with flamethrowers, and so when the poop-flinger came at us we torched him. But he was still running. And so we torched him again, and he kept running. He ran around in a little circle. And he was on fire. And his skin was

melting off him. And there were screams, but they weren't his. There were other poop-flingers inside the poop-tube. They also came running out. They were on fire too. They were much smaller than the first poop-flinger. Half his size. And one really small one.

> *A long beat.*

OWEN

What happened to the prairie dogs?

RODNEY

There were none. I said that already.

OWEN

Right right, you did. My bad, sorry. (*A long beat.*) And so how did you lose your money?

RODNEY

When?

OWEN

You said, before your story. You said it was about nearly losing all your money.

RODNEY

Huh. I did, didn't I?

> *Another long beat.*

> RODNEY *drinks from his wine glass.*

VALERIE

Well I thought it was a marvelous story. Didn't you?

AGNES

Oh yes. I love stories. You are so funny. And your timing is spot on. You should be on stage.

RODNEY

No . . .

AGNES

You really should. You really should be on stage, telling stories. Like that fellow who drowned himself. You should be up there with a desk and a glass of water, telling funny little stories about your life.

RODNEY

I don't have the face for it.

VALERIE

Nonsense. You don't need a face. You don't even need a body. You just need your wits.

RODNEY

I'd have to think about it.

VALERIE

You really should.

AGNES

You really really should.

> JANE FONDA *enters again. She is carrying an enormous tray of Jell-O.*

OWEN

Dessert! Excellent.

RODNEY

Ladies?

> AGNES *and* VALERIE *begin to clear the table, with the help of* JANE FONDA. *When they are done, they turn the table upside down and lay a plastic tarp on the underside.*
>
> *Then* AGNES *and* VALERIE *take off their gowns. They are wearing lingerie underneath. They each do a line of coke off the other's ass.*
>
> *Meanwhile,* RODNEY *and* OWEN *light up cigars. They sit perched forward in their chairs and begin throwing money down.*

JANE FONDA *dumps the Jell-O into the table.* AGNES *and* VALERIE *climb into the Jell-O table.* JANE FONDA *retrieves a whistle.*

AGNES *and* VALERIE *face off.* JANE FONDA *blows the whistle.* AGNES *and* VALERIE *begin to wrestle in the Jell-O, as* RODNEY *and* OWEN *scream from the sidelines and chomp on their cigars, throwing down more money.*

This goes on for quite a while; a full match. Someone wins. The winner of the betting collects his money.

Then JANE FONDA *retrieves two feather pillows. She hands one to* AGNES *and one to* VALERIE. *She blows her whistle.*

AGNES *and* VALERIE *begin to hit each other with the pillows, giggling like little girls.* RODNEY *and* OWEN *watch, eating popcorn.*

The pillows eventually explode into feathers and cover the girls. They giggle like crazy.

RODNEY *and* OWEN *cheer.*

After a moment, VALERIE *becomes aggressive. She beats* AGNES *down with her pillow until* AGNES *is screaming in fear.*

VALERIE *exits.* OWEN *regards* AGNES *in a puddle on the floor, Jell-O-ed and covered in feathers.*

RODNEY *pours his remaining popcorn onto* AGNES *and the floor.* OWEN *and* RODNEY *laugh and slap hands.* RODNEY *exits.*

JANE FONDA *begins to clean up the mess.* OWEN *looks sheepish.*

JANE FONDA
Why are you doing this?

OWEN
I don't know.

JANE FONDA
Pathetic. Wipe that down. Jell-O everywhere. That was your dessert. I made it.

OWEN
I'm, I'm. She's just . . . arrrrgh. You know? I mean how can I even / try to.

JANE FONDA
Shhht!

OWEN
This isn't easy for me, Jane.

JANE FONDA
Stand up.

> OWEN *stands. She approaches him.*

JANE FONDA *(cont.)*
The vigorous and sustained use of your entire imagination will not only tone the muscle of your mind, but will incinerate your worst memories and turn them into fuel. And what good are such toxic recollections if they cannot be converted to sustenance? Hold out your hand.

> JANE FONDA *braces herself.*

JANE FONDA *(cont.)*
I am she, now. The demon.

> OWEN *punches his hand, hard.* JANE FONDA *reacts as though she is being beaten.*

JANE FONDA *(cont.)*
The liar.

> OWEN *punches his hand.* JANE FONDA *reacts.*

JANE FONDA *(cont.)*
The bottomless eater.

> OWEN *punches his hand.* JANE FONDA *reacts.*

JANE FONDA *(cont.)*
The child.

> OWEN *punches his hand.* JANE FONDA *reacts.*

JANE FONDA *(cont.)*
The slut.

> OWEN *punches his hand.* JANE FONDA *reacts.*

JANE FONDA *(cont.)*
The cock-tease.

> OWEN *punches his hand.* JANE FONDA *reacts.*

JANE FONDA *(cont.)*
The vomiter.

> OWEN *punches his hand.* JANE FONDA *reacts.*

JANE FONDA *(cont.)*
The come-hitherer.

> OWEN *punches his hand.* JANE FONDA *reacts.*

JANE FONDA *(cont.)*
The make-you-cry-er.

> OWEN *punches his hand.* JANE FONDA *reacts.*

JANE FONDA *(cont.)*
The hair-sprayer.

> OWEN *punches his hand.* JANE FONDA *reacts.*

JANE FONDA *(cont.)*
The gown-wanter.

> OWEN *punches his hand.* JANE FONDA *reacts.*

JANE FONDA *(cont.)*
The makeup-wearer.

> OWEN *punches his hand.* JANE FONDA *reacts.*

JANE FONDA *(cont.)*
The use-all-the-hot-waterer.

> OWEN *punches his hand.* JANE FONDA *reacts.*

JANE FONDA *(cont.)*
The won't-shut-upper.

> OWEN *punches his hand.* JANE FONDA *reacts.*

JANE FONDA *(cont.)*
The cheater.

> OWEN *punches his hand.* JANE FONDA *finally falls.*

OWEN
Are you okay?

JANE FONDA *(with dignity and grace)*
Of course. It's my job. (*A beat.*) I have something for you.

> JANE FONDA *hands* OWEN *a gown, identical to the one*
> AGNES *wore.*

JANE FONDA *(cont.)*
Now it's your turn.

OWEN
Thank you, Jane . . .

> JANE FONDA *stands and aerobicizes offstage.*

> OWEN *steps into the gown.*

OWEN *(cont.)*
Come on, Owen. Get into it. SLUT SUPREME.

He opens a makeup bag and begins applying makeup, facing forward.

OWEN *(cont.)*

I am so fucking pretty. I am so fucking fucking pretty, yo. Suckas. You wanna suck lemons from my cheeks. I got fuckin' mad pretty on my shit. My pretty is like PROFOUND. It has emissions. Waves of pretty. I'm like a gas burner of pretty. Stick a pot on me I'll make it whistle. Step the fuck off, right, 'cause my pretty will eat your soul. My pretty is a black hole. I am so pretty I drain all the ugly off you and wear it like a swimsuit. GODDAMN AM I PRETTY. Holy fucking shit. You can't stand it. You are like, "She is so pretty I need to BASH her. I need to tear her pubes out. I need to hate on her. That pretty is cancerous. That pretty is a little iced cookie and I need to bite it. That pretty is TOXIC. That pretty boils in my gut, it eats me up, that pretty comes to me at night and scrapes all my tender spots. Soils my boxer briefs. That pretty is FUCKED UP, I need to poke through it with my thumbs, I need to fuck the joy out of that pretty.

I want to kill that pretty. I want to kill that pretty. I want to kill that pretty."

That's what they say about me.

> JANE FONDA *enters. She yanks back a curtain, to reveal . . .*
>
> RODNEY *in rocker tights, big hair, and eyeliner. He is pure rock and roll.*
>
> *Lights and music change . . . we are in a rock-and-roll video circa 1986 . . . smoke, lights, etc. Whitesnake's "Still of the Night" comes on, blasting.*
>
> RODNEY *lip-synchs.*

RODNEY *(mouthing)*
In the still of the night
  I hear the wolf howl, honey
  Sniffing around your door

In the still of the night
I feel my heart beating heavy
Telling me I gotta have more

In the shadow of night
I see the full moon rise
Telling me what's in store,
My heart start aching
My body start a shaking
And I can't take no more

> OWEN *becomes disturbed. Everything stops.*
>
> *Both men face forward for the scene's duration.*
>
> RODNEY *is miked. His voice is seductive, intimate.*

RODNEY *(cont.)*
What's the matter, Owen?

OWEN
I feel strange, Rodney.

RODNEY
About what?

OWEN
I don't know.

RODNEY
Can I do something?

OWEN
Hit me in the face. Get me angry, get me all riled up.

RODNEY
Fist or palm?

OWEN
Fist. No, palm.

OWEN *closes his eyes. He waits. He reacts as though he is being kissed very passionately on the lips—but this should be genuine.*

RODNEY *does as well.*

OWEN *opens his eyes.*

OWEN *(cont.)*
Again.

OWEN *closes his eyes again, and reacts similarly, as does* RODNEY.

OWEN *opens his eyes.*

OWEN *(cont.)*
Try to get your tongue into it.

OWEN *closes his eyes again, and reacts in muted delight.*

He opens his eyes.

OWEN *(cont.)*
Am I blushing?

RODNEY
Yes.

OWEN
One more.

Another kiss.

OWEN *(cont.)*
Okay.

RODNEY
You happy?

OWEN
Yeah.

RODNEY
Jubilant?

OWEN
Yeah, yeah. Thanks. I love you baby. I love you. I love you so much. I want to have a baby. Can we have a baby? I want a baby that looks like you. I want him to have your funny little nose, your eyelashes. I want to make a person who is a product of our love. Can we do that, baby?

RODNEY
Sure.

OWEN
Thank you baby. I love you. I love us.

RODNEY
Sweet.

RODNEY *tumbles offstage.* OWEN *goes into labor.*

OWEN
Jane . . . my water broke . . .

JANE FONDA *rushes in.*

JANE FONDA
Okay, just breathe with me, and two and breathe, and two and push, and two and breathe . . .

OWEN
It hurts . . .

JANE FONDA
. . . and two and again . . . oh, I can see the head . . . okay now push, Owen! Push!

OWEN
It hurts, Jane . . .

JANE FONDA
Come on! You can do it! PUSH!

OWEN
Raaarrgghhhh!!!

> OWEN *gives birth.* JANE FONDA *hands the baby to him.*
>
> OWEN *places the baby to his nipple and nurses the baby in exhausted, blissed-out motherhood.*

JANE FONDA
Well done, Owen! Aw, look at you. You're a mother! You must be over the moon.

OWEN
I couldn't have done it without you, Jane.

JANE FONDA
How are you feeling?

OWEN
Really good.

JANE FONDA
I'm so proud of you. I think you're finally ready.

OWEN
Awesome.

JANE FONDA
Go to it!

> JANE FONDA *begins aerobicizing once again.*
>
> *Lights up on the hotel room again.*
>
> RODNEY, *back in normal slacker gear, is reading the paper and drinking seltzer.*
>
> *Unlike the previous hotel scenes, this room feels authentic and hyperreal. The acting is naturalized.*

OWEN *sits at his computer and begins typing furiously.*

JANE FONDA *enters the hotel room.*

JANE FONDA *(cont.)*
To get the full benefit from the workout you must do it with me from beginning to end without stopping.

JANE FONDA *enters the TV. A workout video on the screen picks up where she left off.*

OWEN *(re: typing)*
Yes yes yes . . . smack that juicy groove . . .

JANE FONDA *(V.O.)*
It is this vigorous and sustained use of your entire body that will not only tone your muscles but will burn up calories, and improve your circulation.

RODNEY *mutes the volume on the workout video.*

RODNEY *(re: the paper)*
Holy shit. They found that guy. The one that blew up that clinic in Atlanta.

OWEN *(not listening)*
Oh?

RODNEY
They found all this shit on him. Gasoline cans, flares, starter fluid, propane tanks, and a pistol. He was on his way to do another.

OWEN
Huh.

RODNEY
Unless those chicks got to him first.

OWEN
Right.

RODNEY
I'll like to fuck them.

OWEN
Huh.

RODNEY
I'd like to fuck them both at once. Put one on each side, then do like a flip and poke. (*He demonstrates.*) Flip, poke, flip, poke. Right? Pump my jizz right in their snatches. Knock 'em both up, then I'll be all, "abort THAT, bitches . . ." I mean what's their fucking deal, right?

OWEN
Their sister got blown up, dude.

RODNEY
How do you know, dude?

OWEN
It's on their blog.

RODNEY
Hey did you know one of them is a dyke? I'm like, "figures."

> RODNEY *is bored. He bends over and sniffs the blanket on his bed.*

RODNEY (*cont.*)
Dude, this place is decent.

OWEN
My uncle works for the chain.

RODNEY
Could get used to this shit. Too bad I'm only on leave for a week.

> OWEN *continues typing,* RODNEY *continues reading the paper. He's bored. He does some aerobics.*

RODNEY *(cont.)*
You hungry?

OWEN
Yeah.

RODNEY
I'm fuckin' hungry, dude.

> RODNEY *picks up the phone and dials.*

RODNEY *(cont.)*
Hi. We'd like some room service please. Eggs benedict, and could you substitute the home fries with like fruit? I dunno, apples, strawberries . . . and send up some coffee and like a, do you have anything chocolate? Okay, that too . . . Owen, what do you want?

OWEN
Do they have Chex?

RODNEY
Do you have Chex? (*To* OWEN.) Raisin Bran and Rice Krispies and granola.

OWEN
Grilled cheese then. With tomatoes and mustard.

RODNEY
Grilled cheese with tomatoes and mustard. Thanks, dude.

> *He hangs up. He is bored. He sniffs the blanket again.*

RODNEY *(cont.)*
Fabric softener. (*Still bored.*) I should piss the bed. Dare me? (*Jumps on the bed and drops his pants.*) Dare me, quick! 'Cause even if you don't I'll still do it . . .

OWEN
I dare you.

> RODNEY *tries to pee.* OWEN *watches him.* RODNEY
> *notices him watching.* OWEN *looks away.*

RODNEY *(cont.)*
Pee, pee . . . Ssssss . . . argh, performance anxiety!!! Wait . . .
there's a trickle . . . (*Pees in the bed.*) I'M PEEING IN THE BED!
I'M PEEING IN THE BED! HOW FUCKING AWESOME IS
THAT?

OWEN
Completely. Dude, please let me finish this, I'm almost done.

> RODNEY *finishes peeing in the bed. He zips up and becomes*
> *immediately bored.*

> *He un-mutes the Jane Fonda video.*

JANE FONDA *(V.O.)*
Head right, two and back, two, and side, two, and front, stretch it
out and to the right, two and reverse, two . . .

RODNEY
Man. She's so fucking PERT. Does she tie that on every morning
or did she grow that way?

OWEN
Pause it for a second.

> RODNEY *pauses the TV.*

RODNEY
What?

OWEN
SHUT THE FUCK UP? PLEASE? a) You see me working here,
b) this room is going to smell like piss all night, c) you promised
you would let me fucking work if I brought you here, and d) you
sound retarded.

> *A beat.* RODNEY *smacks the back of* OWEN'*s head.*

OWEN *(cont.)*
Don't hit me, man.

> RODNEY *smacks the back of* OWEN*'s head again.*

OWEN *(cont.)*
Don't do it again.

> *He does it again.*

> *They scuffle, wrestle, etc, hurling each other playfully around the room.*

OWEN *(cont.)*
Fucker . . .

RODNEY
Pussy . . .

> RODNEY *accidentally slips off the bed and slams his face against something hard.*

OWEN
Whoa. You okay man?

RODNEY
Think so.

> RODNEY *feels the inside of his mouth with his tongue.*

OWEN
Are you bleeding?

RODNEY
Little.

OWEN
Lemme see.

> OWEN *checks the inside of* RODNEY*'s mouth.*

OWEN *(cont.)*
Your got cut on your tooth.

OWEN *takes a piece of ice from the bucket and ices the inside of* RODNEY's *cheek.*

RODNEY
Cold!

OWEN
Don't move.

OWEN *grabs a tissue and blots the inside of* RODNEY's *cheek. Then* OWEN *hands* RODNEY *the mouthwash.*

OWEN *(cont.)*
Rinse, so it won't get infected.

RODNEY *(rinses)*
Faggot.

OWEN
You're the faggot, faggot.

RODNEY
I beg to differ, my faggot.

OWEN
Who's the faggot who just whipped his dick out in front of me?

RODNEY
Who's the faggot with all the Jane Fonda tapes?

OWEN
That's RESEARCH, faggot.

There's a knock on the door. RODNEY *opens the door.*

JANE *(not* JANE FONDA*) stands with a cart of lidded silver platters.*

RODNEY
Wheel it on in . . .

JANE *wheels the cart into the room.*

RODNEY *(cont.)*

Sweetheart, this asshole just pissed in the bed. Could you send someone up to change the sheets?

JANE

Of course.

> JANE *removes the lid from the grilled cheese with a flourish.*

RODNEY

Faaaaancyyyyyyy.

> JANE *removes the lid from the eggs benedict.*

RODNEY *(cont.)*

Oh yeah . . .

> JANE *pours coffee into two cups, holding the coffee pot very*
> *high.* RODNEY *is mesmerized.*

JANE

Sugar?

RODNEY

Three for me, none for him.

> JANE *places three cubes into* RODNEY's *coffee.*

JANE

Black pepper?

RODNEY

Black pepper . . .

> JANE *whips out a pepper grinder from nowhere and expertly*
> *grinds three times over the food.*
>
> *Then she hands him a cloth napkin.*

RODNEY

You are really good at that. What's your name?

JANE
Jane.

RODNEY
Like Fonda!

JANE
Sure.

RODNEY
How long have you been working here, Jane?

JANE
About six months . . .

RODNEY
Do you like it?

JANE
I like it enough.

RODNEY
Do you get benefits and stuff?

JANE
The usual. Heath, 401(k) . . .

RODNEY
I'll bet you see a lot of assholes . . .

JANE
Ah . . .

RODNEY
I'll bet you see a lot of rich fucking assholes who treat you like shit.

JANE
People are generally all right . . .

RODNEY
You're way polite, Jane. Do you get that a lot?

JANE
Once in a while.

RODNEY
I suppose you have to be or else you'd get raped a lot. Are you hungry? I probably won't eat all of this . . .

JANE
I ate, but thank you.

RODNEY
Would you come up later and change the sheets for us?

JANE
I can send up a maid . . .

RODNEY
No, you should come. We want you.

JANE
I don't generally make up the beds . . .

RODNEY
But you will, okay? Because I'm a fucking filthy rapist and I want to get you pregnant.

JANE *(polite and vaguely flirtatious)*
You kiss your mother with that mouth?

RODNEY
Only on her beef curtains . . . Come back in about twenty minutes. We'll be done eating by then, right Owen?

> OWEN *lets out a nervous a laugh.*

RODNEY *(cont.)*
And then you can hang out a little? Although we have no whiskey . . . could you bring some up?

JANE
I'll see what I can do.

RODNEY
Thanks Jane . . .

JANE
It's my job.

RODNEY
Bye.

> JANE *exits.* RODNEY *gleefully grabs his plate and sits on the bed.* OWEN *begins cracking up, but he's kind of scared.*
>
> *They slap hands.*

OWEN
Hoooo!

RODNEY
Now THAT'S dignity.

> RODNEY *begins scarfing his food in huge bites.*

OWEN *(giddy and disturbed)*
"Beef curtains . . ." Holy shit. You are fucking LECHEROUS, dude.

RODNEY
The Rod is in the hizzy! Fuck this is good. Come eat. I hate eating alone. Makes me feel like an addict. That's a good line. You should put it in your screenplay.

OWEN
Taking it all in . . .

> OWEN *types.* RODNEY *eats.*
>
> *A beat.*

RODNEY
Must be nice. To have a calling.

OWEN
You have a calling.

RODNEY
Any fucker with a rifle and conscience could do what I do.

OWEN
I couldn't.

RODNEY
What's it about?

OWEN
Uhhh . . . it's like a "based on." Like "based on a true story."

RODNEY
Like, autobiographical?

OWEN
Uh. Yeah, sorta. But also I'm taking shit from like, the news.

RODNEY
Like what shit?

OWEN
The abortion chicks.

RODNEY
The ones with the blog?

       OWEN *nods.*

RODNEY *(cont.)*
OUTRAGEOUS! Hello, Maestro!

OWEN
Research.

RODNEY
HELLO, Maestro!

OWEN

But it's fictionalized . . . I don't want to get sued.

RODNEY

Pitch it to me.

OWEN

Well, it's early, but . . . and also it might change . . .

RODNEY

"I got Shpeilberg at two, don't have all day . . ."

OWEN

Okay. So like, there's the two chicks. They're like sisters. Or half-sisters. They tell everyone that. And they are SO FUCKING HOT.

RODNEY

Right?

OWEN

So hot that like, your eyebrows get singed around them. Like too hot. And rude. So rude that you like have to put them into a condom. I mean they are SICK. Heavy shit, these two. And one is a bulimic.

RODNEY

Sick.

OWEN

SO sick. And the other is. I dunno. Puerto Rican or something. A real bulldog. Smart, ballsy. Doesn't take shit.

RODNEY

But they're sisters. And they make out occasionally.

OWEN

Yeah, 'cause like, one's a secret lezzy.

RODNEY

The PR.

OWEN

Yeah. AND, she's been fucking the bulimic's husband since they were sixteen.

RODNEY

Right.

OWEN

And they do coke off each other's asses in front of some business-men. At a dinner party. They're strippers. EX-strippers.

RODNEY

You should make the PR girl blind.

OWEN

Why?

RODNEY

And make it like she got fucked over by the two businessmen, which is why she hates men so bad.

OWEN

Which is why she's fucking her sister's husband. Because she secretly hates him too.

RODNEY

But he's really not a bad guy.

OWEN

No. He's just. He has a back problem and a bowel problem. He has to wear a diaper. He fucks her because a) she's SICK hot, and b) he feels bad for her. Because she has jaundice.

RODNEY

She's blind AND has jaundice?

OWEN

Ho, wait. Hepatitis, not jaundice. I get them confused.

RODNEY
Everyone does.

OWEN
So like, then she accuses the husband of raping her, which is how
the bulimic finds out they were fucking.

RODNEY
But he didn't rape her.

OWEN
Nah, dude. There was no fucking rape. YET. But like, okay, so
here's the meat: One night PR is on the pole, right? And she's
workin' it. Good night, bachelor party up front, Japanese suits in
the back . . . In walks Bulimia. And Bulimia's got this LOOK on
her face, like a little . . .

OWEN *trembles his bottom lip.*

RODNEY
The trembly lip! HATE that shit.

OWEN *(girl voice)*
"Our baby sister got capped," she says. "Some neo-con stuffed his
trunk full of shit and drove up outside this clinic. BOOOOM.
They found part of her hanging from a telephone pole three blocks
away."

RODNEY
The armpit . . .

OWEN
What? No man, like a, like a shoe or. But so they stand there, and
they DON'T EVEN CRY. No crying. Not even a whimper. DIG-
NITY SUPREME. The PR just kind of turns to the camera and
looks us dead in the eye and says, "IT'S ON." (*A beat.*) So PR's like
the mastermind of the whole enterprise. She a) makes the blog,
b) gets the camera, and c) buys the gun. She writes this long-ass
manifesto—all this shit about her uterus, the Internet, the FCC,

et cetera. They pool all their stripper money together and procure a hoopty. They motor from state to state and show up to all these pro-life conventions looking like Grade A Tail. They bring home the sloppy dudes. Fuck 'em if they can get wood. And THEN.

   OWEN *makes gun-fingers and pulls the trigger.*

OWEN *(cont.)*
BANG! (*Girl voice.*) "Keep your laws off my fucking body!!"

RODNEY
Fucking CHILLING, man. There's a market for that shit.

OWEN
There's TOTALLY a market for this shit! These bitches with the blog, they're like female Dukes of Hazzard. Taking the law into their own hands. (*Girl voice.*) "Don't fuck with me suckas or I will cut you!"

RODNEY
Dude. There's your title.

OWEN
I already have a title. (*Marquee title.*) AN UNBEARABLE PROPOSITION.

RODNEY
I like it. I like it.

OWEN
And there's more! So one night they're in Mississippi at this convention. Everything is swell. Dude's getting sloppy, spilling Wild Turkey on his pants. They make the transaction. PR goes to her car to get change. Dude follows her out and BEATS THE LIVING CRAP OUT OF HER. I mean she is TOTALLY fucked up. Black eye, lip hanging. But of course she looks so fucking hot. So she's there in the hospital, all fucked up and hot. And THEN there's rape. Lots of it. The orderly rapes the PR. And then the doctor. And then a male nurse. It's one big bang-fest. And the dudes feel fucking AWFUL about it. But the PR lezzy NEVER

FUCKING CRIES. She stands all shaky and bloody and dignified with her chin turned up, and then the doctor who was the last to have her—

RODNEY
A neurosurgeon!

OWEN
—he can't look her in the face, because this is like his greatest downfall, he's like "Tragically Flawed Dude," hubris and all that, he's like Hamlet, right, and he thinks about how in med school they never prepared you for the fuckable lost ones, you know the ones who don't actually look into your eyes but through you as if you were a pile of ash because of all the fucked up ruinous shit from their past, a molesty stepdad or white slavery or whatever, so they gotta exact some foul revenge on you because you are a) in the way and b) looking like someone who needs to be taken down, and so they spread their damage on a shiny silver platter and say "Munch it, baby," and you just can't stop yourself because nothing tastes more delicious than a steaming hot mound of damage. (*A beat.*) So the doctor is thinking this shit, and then he thinks of his wife at home and his two sons, they're twins and they wear matching baseball pajamas to bed, and his wife lost all the baby weight the second they popped out because she didn't want to be one of those lard-asses in the Key Food wearing sweatpants and a hairnet, and like she never leaves the house without makeup, and all his golf buddies are like "How the fuck did YOU land such a tasty beverage?" and he gets fake-mad at them but he is secretly so fucking proud because he's the only one of them who still gets regular blowjobs, and when he goes home that night she'll be waiting for him on the porch drinking a glass of white wine and smoking a J, and she'll offer him a hit and ask him how his day was, and at that moment—AT THAT MOMENT he'll conjure that bloody fucking broken cunty bitch in her little hospital gown and her eyes made of ash and he will release her into the evening air and she will never enter his mind again. (*A beat.*)

So this neurosurgeon is finishing up his rape, and he's pulling up his scrubs and thinking about his wife and not looking at PR, and PR tries to say something all significant like a supreme like philosophical sentence or whatever, but he whispers "Just go." And walks out. And she's left there alone in the room. And she stands up all wobbly on her colt legs, and her hospital gown is all open and you can see her titties, and then Bulimia shows up. And she looks at PR, all fucked up and raped. And she's like, wait a second. I'm still sore about PR fucking my husband. But what she DOESN'T know is—get this—is that PR fucked her husband to get the cizash for their baby sister's abortion!

RODNEY
Joan of Arc!

OWEN
And Bulimia DOESN'T KNOW! So Bulimia steps out of the room to quote-unquote "Get a Diet Coke," and comes back with a gat. BAM.

RODNEY
Right in the face.

OWEN
Never saw her coming.

RODNEY
Blind motherfucking whore.

OWEN
Um wait. She's not blind. She's just normal. (*He types a little.*) And dykey. A little dykey.

RODNEY
Not man-dykey . . .

OWEN
No, normal. Wears dresses and thongs but likes to fuck girls.

RODNEY
It's so topical.

OWEN
Right? Some fucked-up shit chicks go through. Rape, and babies, and stripping, and being objectified by the media . . .

A small beat.

RODNEY
What are you, a FEMINIST?

OWEN *(genuine)*
I want to write a movie my mom will be proud of. My mom is a strong fucking woman, homes. Every time one of her ex-husbands dumps on her, she takes it like a pro. Chin up. Pure class. Table-cloths and linens. That's my mom.

RODNEY
Right on.

OWEN
She's my hero, man. And you know who her hero is?

RODNEY
No clue.

OWEN *(points to TV)*
Hanoi. Fucking. Jane.

RODNEY *(delighted)*
Traitorous commie bitch. Full circle, dude!

OWEN
Precision!

RODNEY
Minty fresh! That's beautiful.

OWEN
Yeah? You weren't bored or anything?

RODNEY

Yeah, a little. Yo, I heard she did threesomes with her French hus-band. AGAINST HER WILL.

OWEN

How do you force someone to do a threesome?

RODNEY

She didn't WANT to, but she loved him so much she did it any-way. That's one special female.

OWEN

Dignity, man. "Don't fuck with me. I'll do what you want, but don't fuck with me." It's about self-respect.

RODNEY

Right. "How can I respect you when you don't respect yourself?"

OWEN

Exactly. (*A beat.*) I'm glad you're here, man.

RODNEY

Me too. Want your grilled cheese?

OWEN

I'm starving.

> *A beat as* OWEN *eats.*

OWEN *(cont.)*

Yo. I'm thinking about putting the war in my screenplay.

RODNEY

Yeah?

OWEN

I wanna juxtapose the crap in the Middle East with the war on women's bodies. Not sure how yet. It's an experiment.

RODNEY

You should put in that fucked up shit I told you.

OWEN
I did.

> *A beat.*

RODNEY
You did? About the thirteen-year-old chick?

OWEN
No, man. The other shit. The cave with two entrances. Poop-tube.

RODNEY
Oh. (*A beat.*) You should put in the other thing, too.

OWEN
The . . . the . . .

RODNEY
Because it was fucked up. And no one's talking about it.

OWEN
Man, I / don't

RODNEY (*quietly*)
All of us, man. One after another. She just laid there. Never cried, not once. Then we shoved a grenade in her snatch. Pulled the fucking pin. (*A long beat.*) Who's gonna tell the tales? You, man. (*A long beat.*) Because I'm dyslexic.

OWEN
I'll think about it.

RODNEY
That's all I ask. (*A beat.*) Am I in it?

OWEN
Um . . . kinda . . .

RODNEY
Damn! Academy Awards! Roll up in the Bentley, be all, "S'up, Betties, it's The Rod" . . . do I get to hump anyone?

OWEN
A corpse.

RODNEY
Whoa. I don't like that.

OWEN
But it isn't really you, dude. Like I'll be working it, trying to make the females into human beings, and then I'll fucking lose it. So I stick us in there for a while until I get it back.

RODNEY
Does it work?

OWEN
Fuck, yeah!

RODNEY
Process. I like it. Using models. You're an artist. I never knew any artists. Faggot.

OWEN
Suck me.

RODNEY
Who's the bulimic?

OWEN *says nothing.*

RODNEY *(cont.)*
Not Agnes.

OWEN *says nothing.*

RODNEY *(cont.)*
That ratty piece of neighborhood trash?

OWEN *says nothing.*

RODNEY *(cont.)*
That's cool, that's cool. She's like your muse.

OWEN
Whatever.

> OWEN *finishes his sandwich.* RODNEY *slaps him on the back.*

RODNEY
Yo. You are WRITING THAT SHIT. GO WRITE THAT SHIT, man.

OWEN
Fo' shizzle.

> OWEN *returns to typing.* RODNEY *returns to the Jane Fonda video.*

OWEN *(cont.)*
Turn it up. I wanna hear her.

RODNEY
Inspiration. Riiiiight. Hello, Maestro!

OWEN
Hell-LO!

> RODNEY *turns up the volume.* OWEN *types. Lights change.*

> JANE FONDA *appears, dressed in her Hanoi Jane gear.*

> OWEN *remains on stage, typing throughout. He mouths the words that the girls shout, getting more and more excited by the minute.*

JANE FONDA
Men.
  You think you can do whatever you want with me, think again.
  You think that I'm so delicate?
  You think you have to care for me?
  You throw me to the ground
  You think I break?

(Throws herself to the ground, aerobic-style.)
You think I can't get up again?
　You think I can't get up again?

　　　JANE FONDA *gets up.*

JANE FONDA *(cont.)*
You think I need a man to save my life?

　　　She throws herself to the ground again.

JANE FONDA *(cont.)*
I don't need a man!
　I don't need a man!

　　　*She gets up, does some aerobics, and throws herself to the ground
　　　again and again as she yells.*

　　　OWEN *types.*

JANE FONDA *(cont.)*
These men can fuck themselves!
　These men are leeches
　these men are cheaters
　these rapists,
　these politicians,
　these war mongers,

　　　She is throwing herself to the ground over and over.

　　　*Music kicks in over this— maybe a techno version of J. S. Bach's
　　　"Sleepers Awake!" from Cantata No. 140 (although I'm sure
　　　there's a better and more appropriate song choice out there)—
　　　and, as she hits the ground over and over, she repeats her same
　　　litany as she does.* AGNES *and* VALERIE *enter wearing
　　　military fatigues and watch her.*

　　　AGNES *joins in and starts throwing herself to the ground
　　　aerobically and synchronously so that it is a choreographed
　　　aerobics piece of the two women.*

VALERIE *watches*. OWEN *types*.

JANE FONDA and AGNES
These faggots,
   these soldiers,
   these impregnators,
   these golfers,
   neo-cons,
   neurosurgeons,
   screenplay writers!

> *Now* AGNES *starts to yell, too, simultaneously with* JANE
> FONDA, *on top of her words, as both of them continue to
> throw themselves to the ground over and over.*

> OWEN *types*.

AGNES
These men!
   These men!
   All I wanted was a man who could be a man
   a man who wouldn't cry
   a man who would let me drink
   a man who would fight for my honor

JANE FONDA
These men should be eliminated!
   These men should be snuffed out!
   Who needs a man?
   Who needs a man?
   I'll make it on my own.
   I'm an autonomous person!
   I'm an independent person!
   I am frank and dignified!
   I can do what I want!
   I can be who I am!
   And I can also be who you want me to be!

Hey!
I don't actually want men to be eliminated!
I just said that so you will respect me!
I'll say anything you want
And do anything you want
Just so you'll respect me!

AGNES *(still yelling simultaneously with JANE FONDA)*
And I don't think it's wrong
   to drink a little sometimes
   and wear perfume
   and keep myself skinny
   to like my clothes
   and think they're sexy
   and wear short skirts
   that blow up in the wind
   I don't think it's wrong
   for several men to love me at once
   to like to touch me
   and listen to me
   and talk to me
   and write me notes
   and give me flowers
   because I like men
   I like men
   And, I like to be hit sometimes.

> *And, finally,* **VALERIE** *joins in too, until all three women are yelling their words over the loud music and throwing themselves to the ground over and over.*
>
> OWEN *types.*

ALL THREE WOMEN TOGETHER
Why can't a man
   be more like a woman?

VALERIE *(Puerto Rican accent)*
I don't know what I'm doing here.
  I don't want a man to be more like a woman.
  I just want a woman:
  emotionally available
  able to process
  to deal with her feelings
  to speak from the heart
  to say what she means.
  To not violate me
  to not violate me
  to not violate me
  or hit me
  or shoot me in the face.

AGNES
I don't want a man I can hit.
  I don't want a pussy.
  I don't want a woman.

JANE FONDA
I have self-respect.
  I have dignity.
  I want a woman.
  If you want me to have a woman.

ALL THREE WOMEN TOGETHER
I am not conflicted!
  I know exactly who I am!
  I know exactly what I want!

> *The women then tear their fatigues off and begin pole dancing and rubbing up against one another.*
>
> OWEN *stops typing a moment and watches, as . . .*
>
> RODNEY *enters in army fatigues. He pulls out a rifle. He executes them, one by one.*

Lights change, to a soft flickering light. Bombs can be heard exploding outside.

A hospital room.

VALERIE is lying in her bed, all beaten up in her hospital gown. She is the picture of dignity. Her chin is high.

This scene is heightened in the style of a sweeping wartime epic, underscored by music. This is OWEN's film.

AGNES enters, dramatically. She wears a burka.

VALERIE still has a Puerto Rican accent, but now with some "Middle Eastern" mixed in.

VALERIE
Oh hello, Nouri al-Maliki Mahmoud . . . have you come for my daily sponge bath?

AGNES
I am not Nouri al-Maliki Mahmoud . . .

VALERIE
Are you with the resistance?

AGNES
I was, once . . . a long long time ago . . .

VALERIE
Agnes? Could it be you?

A weighted pause. She whips off her burka.

AGNES
Yes.

AGNES *embraces* VALERIE. VALERIE *winces in pain.*

AGNES *(cont.)*
Dear God, what have they done to you?

VALERIE
The boys here have been a little, how shall I say . . . overly friendly.

AGNES
They didn't. They wouldn't!

VALERIE
They have. Many times over.

AGNES
They will pay for this . . .

VALERIE
Oh Agnes . . . save your fury for the battlefield. So rarely do they see a kind face here, a kind soul. A kind heart. These are broken men, Agnes. Men who have lost their spirit. There is no one left to give them what they want, so they feel they must take it. Please don't blame them . . . blame the war.

AGNES
This infernal war!

> *A huge shattering bomb explodes nearby. The women cover their heads. Pieces of plaster fall from the ceiling.*

VALERIE
Oh Agnes . . . you must get out of here before it's too late . . .

AGNES
But what about you?

VALERIE
I know I won't get out alive. I've made my peace.

> AGNES *hurls herself onto the bed and begins to weep.*

VALERIE *(cont.)*
Don't cry for me, my dear sister . . .

AGNES
You don't understand . . . I came here to kill you . . .

Another huge bomb explodes outside. More plaster falls.

VALERIE
What do you mean?

AGNES
All those years you were sleeping with my husband . . . I swore I would get revenge . . . but then we formed the resistance . . . and I believed we were working toward something much bigger . . . but then the resistance fell apart . . . we are losing the war, Valerie . . . all around us is in ruins . . . nothing but despair and heartache . . .

VALERIE
Then do it, Agnes . . . kill me.

> AGNES *pulls out a gun. She holds it up to shoot* VALERIE, *her arm trembling.*

VALERIE *(cont.)* *(supremely dignified)*
Go on. Pull the trigger.

AGNES
I . . . can't . . .

> *She drops the gun and flees to* VALERIE. *They stare into each other's eyes a moment. They kiss passionately.*

> OWEN *enters in a lab coat with a rolling tray of food.*

> AGNES *scrambles to get her burka back on.*

AGNES *(cont.)*
Oh . . .

OWEN
Sorry for the interruption . . .

> OWEN *hands* VALERIE *a bedpan. She tucks it under herself and pees, all with great pain, then hands it back to* OWEN.

OWEN *(cont.)*
Lunchtime.

> OWEN *uncovers a little plastic tray.*

AGNES
Thank goodness. I'm starving.

VALERIE
But Agnes . . . you don't eat . . .

AGNES *(hurt)*
You don't know me any more, Valerie . . .

> OWEN *uncovers another little plastic tray.*

AGNES *(cont.)*
Grilled cheese . . .

OWEN
With mustard.

> OWEN *pours coffee into two cups, holding the coffee pot very high.* AGNES *is mesmerized.*

AGNES
You are really good at that.

VALERIE
Agnes . . .

> AGNES *ignores* VALERIE *and flirts mercilessly with* OWEN.

> OWEN *begins to sing to himself as he pours.*

OWEN *(singing)*
Everybody loves a baby
  That's why I'm in love with you,
  Pretty Baby, Pretty Baby

  Sugar?

AGNES

Three for me, none for her.

VALERIE

Agnes, please . . .

> OWEN *places three cubes into* AGNES's *coffee.*

OWEN *(singing)*

And I'd like to be your sister, brother
  Dad and mother too,
  Pretty Baby, Pretty Baby.

> *He whips out a paper napkin and hands it to her.*

AGNES

What song is that?

OWEN

I don't know . . . my mother used to sing it to me.

AGNES

What's your name?

OWEN

Owen.

AGNES

I knew a fellow named Owen once . . .

OWEN

Did you.

AGNES

He was a bit of a pansy. He let me hit him. And he cried all the time. His penis was shaped like a cashew. He was in love with his best friend. He called him "The Rod." Isn't that hilarious?

> *A bruised* VALERIE *begins to leave the bed.*

VALERIE *(wounded)*
I'm going outside for a Diet Coke . . .

> OWEN *suddenly grabs the gun that* AGNES *dropped earlier and aims it at* VALERIE.

OWEN
Do not leave the fucking room.

AGNES
Oh my God . . . You're one of THEM . . .

OWEN
That's right, American gypsy . . .

> *He aims the gun at* AGNES *and grips* VALERIE *by her throat.*

OWEN *(cont.)*
You two ladies thought you could defeat us with your little "resistance." Well we've had you in our sights for a long time. And payback is a total bitch. *(To* AGNES.*)* I advise you to watch carefully, Agnes. *(To* VALERIE.*)* I'm going to rape you now, Valerie.

> VALERIE *nods. With dignity, she leans back and spreads her legs.*

AGNES
NOOO!

VALERIE
It's all right, Agnes . . .

> OWEN *prepares himself for his rape.*

AGNES
Please . . .

OWEN
Please what?

AGNES
Please don't rape my sister . . .

OWEN
As much as I love to hear you beg, I AM going to rape your sister, Agnes. I'm going to rape her with my enormous cock. My enormous, completely straight cock that does not at all resemble any kind of salted nut.

> AGNES *struggles to remove her burka.*

OWEN *(cont.)*
Keep the fucking burka on.

> OWEN *begins to rape* VALERIE *as* AGNES *watches in horrified silence.*
>
> *AGNES begins to cry.*

OWEN *(cont.)*
Look, your sister is crying! But you haven't cried once, Valerie. You are so dignified. You won't cry, will you?

VALERIE
No.

OWEN
I know you won't. You have too much class for that. You are dignified and heroic.

VALERIE
Thank you.

OWEN
You're welcome.

> OWEN *continues his rape. He climaxes.*

OWEN *(cont.)*
I'm done raping you now, Valerie. You did very well.

VALERIE
Thank you.

OWEN
Now I'm going to stick a grenade in your vagina and I'm going to pull the pin. Okay?

VALERIE
Okay.

OWEN
Okay.

AGNES
You bastard!

> *She charges* OWEN. OWEN *smacks her down with the gun.*
>
> *Then he removes a grenade from his pocket.*

OWEN
What I do here today, I do for the good of my country, my people, and all mankind.

> *He sticks the grenade into* VALERIE's *vagina. He closes his eyes.*

OWEN (*quietly*)
Goodnight, Maestro.

> *He pulls the pin. All three cringe.*
>
> *Darkness.*
>
> *After a long moment, a single light rises upon . . .*
>
> *A chair. A bottle of water. A microphone.*
>
> *Another long moment.* OWEN *enters, wearing a tweed jacket and glasses. He smiles and waves at the audience, mouthing the words "thank you" a few times. He is gracious and humble.*

Then he takes his seat. Smiles and waves again. Takes a sip of his water. Smiles and nods. Laughs at something we don't hear. He leans into the mike.

OWEN *(cont.)*
Except when I'm sober.

He laughs, then waves the joke away.

OWEN *(cont.)*
'K, ah, I only have a few minutes, so . . .

Takes another sip of his water. Squints and points to someone in the audience.

OWEN *(cont.)*
Yes.

Leans forward, straining, as though he is listening to something someone is saying. He nods and then leans into the mike.

OWEN *(cont.)*
Ah. Great. I'm so glad you asked that question. Remember that huge story last year about the two girls who'd go to pro-life conventions and kill men, then write about it on their blog? I started writing about them, initially. But then I became fascinated by the war. And so the girls kind of morphed into this legion of pro-Iraq feminist insurgents. And it went from there.

Shields his eyes and points to someone else in the audience.

OWEN *(cont.)*
You, in the hat.

He cups his ear, listening, nodding, sipping on his water.

He leans into the mike.

OWEN *(cont.)*
Well I wouldn't say I have a "bleak" outlook on life, per se. But I do think humans are a pretty cruel bunch . . . As I see it, I'm not

creating reprehensible characters, I'm merely giving voice to the unspoken.

Scans the audience and points to someone else.

OWEN *(cont.)*
You, yes. (*He listens. Into the mike.*) I certainly don't expect everyone to love it. This kind of work is polarizing. Some people don't want to see the truth. But my question to them is, why is "truth" so controversial? It's like a flock of geese . . . when you see them from afar in a field, they look great, they look beautiful, but if you go out in the field, it's covered with shit. And the geese are looking down at that shit saying, "Where did that come from?" Well we are knee-deep in it right now, as a country. And THAT'S the truth. Like it or not.

Scans the audience and points to someone else.

OWEN *(cont.)*
Okay, you. Hi. (*He listens. Into the mike.*) Yes. My mother. She's sitting right there, actually. Hey, mom. She's so cute.

> *He waves and laughs. Scans the audience and points to someone else.*

> *He listens.*

OWEN *(cont.) (into the mike)*
Um, gosh. I never know how to answer that. Um, Jean-Luc Godard is an influence, definitely. Scorsese, uh . . . Mel Gibson, believe it or not . . . Woody Allen, David Lynch . . . I could go on.

Scans the audience and points to someone else.

OWEN *(cont.)*
Yes, in the back. (*He listens. Into the mike.*) That's kind of you to say. But honestly? I don't think of them as "female" characters. I think of them as people. I'm an observer of the human condition, irregardless of gender. I'm "gender-blind," as they say.

OWEN *acknowledges someone offstage as though they are telling him his time is almost up. He scans the audience and points to someone else.*

OWEN *(cont.)*
One last question, yes.

He sips his water and listens.

This question has clearly blown his mind. He's at a loss. He leans into the mike. He opens his mouth to speak. He closes it. He opens it again. He closes it. He opens it again.

This goes on for a bit.

Black out.

End of play.

ACKNOWLEDGMENTS

I would like to express my deepest gratitude to the following individuals and organizations, without whose guidance, artistry, patience, and support these plays would not exist:

- my most rare and treasured collaborators—the directors Kip Fagan, Daniella Topol, and Paul Willis

- the generous and indefatigable folks at the Women's Project, the Cherry Lane Theatre, Circle X, Rattlestick Playwrights' Theater, and Clubbed Thumb, notably Angelina Fiordellisi, James King, Julie Crosby, Megan Carter, David van Asselt, Sandra Coudert, Timothy Wright, Jen Kays, Maria Striar, and Diana Konopka—brave people making scary, visceral, essential theater

- the incredible staff at New Dramatists, including Todd London, Emily Morse, Joel K. Ruark, Jennie Greer, John Steber, Ron Riley, Erin Detrick, and Morgan Allen, who allowed me to pester them endlessly for access to programs and rehearsal space and lodging and child-care advice and anything else one might imagine

- the freakishly talented playwrights of 13P

- my playwright muses near and distant, including Caryl Churchhill, Sam Shepard, Harold Pinter, Samuel Beckett, Edward Albee, Maria Irene Fornes, Lisa D'Amour, Caridad Svich, Naomi Iizuka, Erik Ehn, Mac Wellman, David Adjimi, and Jason Grote

- the hordes of artists and craftsfolk who have at some point found their feet planted inside one or more of these plays, including

Suli Holum, Birgit Huppuch, Sam Gold, Heidi Schreck, Jenny Morris, Hannah Cabbell, Carla Harting, Sheri Graubert, Polly Carl, Brooke O'Hara, Brendan Connelly, Amy Mueller, Bill Coelius, Dan Illian, Max Jenkins, Jeff Biehl, Sam Wright, Robin Lord Taylor, Andrew Dolan, Mark Shanahan, Laura Heisler, Teddy Bergman, Gibson Frazier, Danny Manley, Matt Maher, Mather Zickel, Reed Birney, Adam Farabee, Darren Pettie, Joel van Liew, Alex Anfanger, Maria Dizzia, Ana Reeder, Rebecca Henderson, David Brooks, Sarah Leonard, Matthew Macquire, Polly Lee, Danny Mastriogiorgio, Linsay Firman, Marya Mazor, Jackie Wright, Lia Aprile, Flora Diaz, Suzanne Agins, Charles Borland, Danielle Skraastad, Christina Bennett Lind, Jesse Camp, Amy Ryan, Shana Dowdeswell, Chris Kipiniak, Alana Dietze, Olivia Henry, Silas Weir Mitchell, Alina Phelan, Daniel Aukin, Rob Campbell, Elizabeth Waterston, Dana Eskelson, Ronete Levenson, Jason Patric, Joseph Gomez, Lisa Joyce, Greg Keller, Annie McNamara, Danielle Slavick, Chad Beckim, Molly Pearson, Erica Gould, Sharon Freedman, Cynthia Silver, Di Johnston, Vincent Madero, Greg Keller, Alexander Alioto, Sarah Malkin, Jessa Sherman, Paola Grande, Gregory Moss, S. Parker Leventer, Travis York, Lula Graves, Alissa Ford, Adrien-Alice Hansel, Rebecca Hart, Cory Hinkle, Rory Lipede, Amanda White, Deb Fink, Juliet Tanner, Davina Cohen, Anil Margsahayam, Anthony Nemirovsky, Adam Greenfield, and anyone else I'm forgetting

- my wonderful theater agent, Seth Glewen—a gentleman and a killer

- support organizations such as the Playwrights Foundation, the Playwrights' Center, NYFA, NYSCA, the MAP Fund, the NEA, the Rockefeller Foundation, LMCC, TCG, the William Inge Center, the Millay Colony, South Coast Rep, Soho Rep, the Susan Smith Blackburn Prize, the Mrs. Giles Whiting Foundation, Playwrights Horizons, and all others who helped fund, house, develop, and sustain these plays

- my dear friends Kenyatta Cheese, Kirstin Ohrt, Patricia Tilburg, Brian Lang, Melissa Riker, Brent Popolizio, Kristen Palmer, Adam Szymkowicz, Deron Bos, Hilary Ketchum, Chris DeWan, Sarah Hart, Mike Daisey, Jean-Michele Gregory, Sherry Kramer, Jessica Kubzansky, Danny Halstead, and Jay Jennings

- and Denise Oswald, my awesome publisher

Thank you so so so much, gang. I am absolutely indebted to you all, and cannot express my appreciation enough.

Printed in the United States
by Baker & Taylor Publisher Services